EAR TRAINING
A Technique for Listening

Third Edition

EAR TRAINING
A Technique for Listening

Bruce Benward
University of Wisconsin—Madison

wcb
Wm. C. Brown Publishers
Dubuque, Iowa

wcb group

Wm. C. Brown, Chairman of the Board
Mark Falb, President and Chief Executive Officer

wcb
Wm. C. Brown Publishers,
College Division

G. Franklin Lewis, Executive Vice-President, General Manager
E. F. Jogerst, Vice-President, Cost Analyst
George Wm. Bergquist, Editor in Chief
Edward G. Jaffe, Executive Editor
Beverly Kolz, Director of Production
Chris C. Guzzardo, Vice-President, Director of Sales and
  Marketing
Bob McLaughlin, National Sales Manager
Marilyn A. Phelps, Manager of Design
Colleen A. Yonda, Production Editorial Manager
Faye M. Schilling, Photo Research Manager

Book Team
Editor, Karen Speerstra
Assistant Editor, Carol Mills
Editorial Assistant, Sharon R. Nesteby
Permissions Editor, Vicki Krug
Product Manager, Marcia Stout

Consulting Editor
Frederick W. Westphal
California State University, Sacramento

Cover photo © Geoffrey Gove.

Library of Congress Catalog Card Number: 86–72597

ISBN 0–697–03623–5

Printed in the United States of America
10 9 8 7 6 5 4 3 2

ACKNOWLEDGMENTS

Kenneth C. Slavett
Appalachian State University, NC

Larry Willcoxon
Tarrant County Junior College, TX
South Campus

Jonathan J. Wills
Portland State University, OR

Kenley Inglefield
Bowling Green State University, OH

Arthur S. Danner
West Los Angeles College, CA

Ronald A. Hough
Midwestern State University, TX

Wm. John Hooper, III
James Madison University, VA

Roy W. Carroll
Loras College, IA

Contents

Unit 8   91

Unit 9   103

Unit 10   117

PREFACE

If you enjoy performing and listening to music, you will find this text equally satisfying and productive. However, unlike in some of your previous experiences with music, you will be asked to apply conscious thought and concentration in identifying the myriad patterns and diverse tonal shapes that are the very heart of music. If the idea of critical listening is new to you, remember that the vast array of tonal configurations found in music comprises the basic material of the art, and the ingredients are digested to produce aesthetic pleasure. Thus, listening for recognition of musical devices and structures should not hinder aesthetic enjoyment, but should, on the other hand, enhance it considerably.

Before commencing this book, I set forth several goals to be achieved in writing it. Among these were:

The book must contain a sufficient number of exercises on any one topic for students to obtain a solid grasp of the material.

If this is not done, the book will be simply an introduction to problems without adequate means to solve them. It must contain exercises for classroom presentation and extra work for outside practice.

The book must begin at the beginning.

The most basic elements of music are intervals, simple melodies, simple triads, scales, and simple rhythms. Most students entering a career in music know these ingredients from sight, but few know them from sound. Until the basics are mastered, the complex idioms of composition cannot be undertaken.

The book should be sufficiently diverse to remove the tedium faced when students solve the same problem in the same way day in and day out.

Included are a variety of approaches to ear training. To mention a few, some exercises include simple dictation, some indicate errors to be found, and others require more complex written responses.

The book must be practical.

Each series of exercises must develop some kind of practical skill that will be of genuine value in professional life later on.

When you have successfully completed this text, you will have acquired the following skills that are essential for any well-equipped musician:

1. You will be able to identify all intervals quickly and accurately. At first, the instructor will play the intervals slowly, allowing you time for an accurate assessment, but later on he or she will increase the tempo of interval dictation so you will learn to identify intervals in a split second. You will be happily surprised at your progress provided that your practice is intensive and regular.
2. After hearing a melody two or three times, you will be able to write it on score paper. The book starts with fairly simple melodies and progresses to those more complex. If you keep up with the class at every step of the way, the more difficult melodies will be taken in stride. Since a large majority of the melodies are taken from printed compositions, you will at the same time become familiar with a considerable amount of music literature.
3. You will be able to hear and name chord progressions. These chords in a series will be explained thoroughly by the instructor as preparation for the actual listening. Sing the chords you are to identify and make sure you know what you are listening for *before* the exercise starts. At first the instructor will play the progressions very slowly to give you time to distinguish each individual chord and its unique sound. Later on, after experience, your ear will begin to group sounds in a way that makes identification much easier. Here again,

only listening itself will help—verbal descriptions are useless.

4. You will be able to distinguish rhythmic patterns, at first quite short and simple. But, as your ear begins to "think," you will discover that your capacity for more complex rhythms is increasing rapidly.

5. After much emphasis on the fundamentals, the book progresses to the integration of all previously learned material. You will begin to listen to entire phrases, no longer with the goal of writing down the notes, but to grasp the larger patterns of notes that form such compositional devices as sequences, rhythmic repetitions, harmonic rhythm, phrase extensions, cadence types, and so on. If your progress is steady and successful to this point, you will find the aural analysis of even larger sections or complete compositions quite within your grasp.

Intelligent listening is the most important thing a musician does. No matter what high level of dexterity and accuracy is achieved with an instrument or voice, success is inevitably limited and regulated by the ability of the ear to discriminate and guide the musical performance. It is thus toward the maximum in aural perception that this book is dedicated.

UNIT 1

Melody 1A

Scales: Major and Harmonic Minor Scales

Your instructor will play melodies based on major and minor scales.

1. Before listening to the melodies, play **major** and **harmonic minor scales** on your instrument or piano until you know their sound well.
2. Sing the same scales until you can sing both major and harmonic minor from any given **pitch.**
3. Now, listen to the melody once and capture the last pitch in your mind by matching its pitch immediately after it is played. All the melodies in this section end on the **tonic** (first) pitch of the scale.
4. Try to reconstruct the scale by remembering the notes of the melody and forming the scale from your recollections.
5. You may need a couple of hearings before you have all the pitches in your mind.
6. If you prepared items 1 and 2 (above) well, you should be able to recognize whether the scale is major or harmonic minor.
7. Finally, circle the correct answer (major or minor).

1. MAJOR MINOR	6. MAJOR MINOR	11. MAJOR MINOR	16. MAJOR MINOR
2. MAJOR MINOR	7. MAJOR MINOR	12. MAJOR MINOR	17. MAJOR MINOR
3. MAJOR MINOR	8. MAJOR MINOR	13. MAJOR MINOR	18. MAJOR MINOR
4. MAJOR MINOR	9. MAJOR MINOR	14. MAJOR MINOR	19. MAJOR MINOR
5. MAJOR MINOR	10. MAJOR MINOR	15. MAJOR MINOR	20. MAJOR MINOR

Melody 1B

Scales: Scalewise Melodies with Errors

Each exercise consists of a short **melody** that your instructor will play. Each melody as played contains two pitch errors—pitches with letter names different from those printed in your workbook.

1. Before listening to each melody, sing it over in your mind—or out loud if you are working outside of class.
2. Make sure you know what the melody sounds like as it is shown on the page. This is very important.
3. Each melody as played contains two pitch errors—pitches that have letter names different from those printed.
4. The first pitch of each melody is correct, so you will always have a point of reference.
5. As you listen to the melody played, concentrate on your original version as you sang it.
6. When you hear a melody pitch that surprises you, circle the number above it.
7. Check your answers while you hear the melody again.

Melody 1C

Melodic Dictation: Scalewise (Conjunct Diatonic) Melodies

Each exercise consists of a short melodic phrase. Listen to the phrase as it is played. Complete the phrase on the staff in notation.

1. As you listen to each melody the first time, try to memorize it immediately—in its entirety.
2. Do *not* write anything on paper yet! You will learn almost nothing by trying to write too early.
3. Sing as much of the melody as you can from first hearing before you listen to it again.
4. Continue to listen until you can hear all the pitches. Sing the entire melody from memory.
5. Only after you have the entire melody memorized should you attempt to write anything on paper!
6. Observe that when you have the melody memorized, you can slow it down sufficiently to write the notes on the staff as you sing (or preferably think).
7. Write the melody on the staff in music notation.

*(R) means recorded.

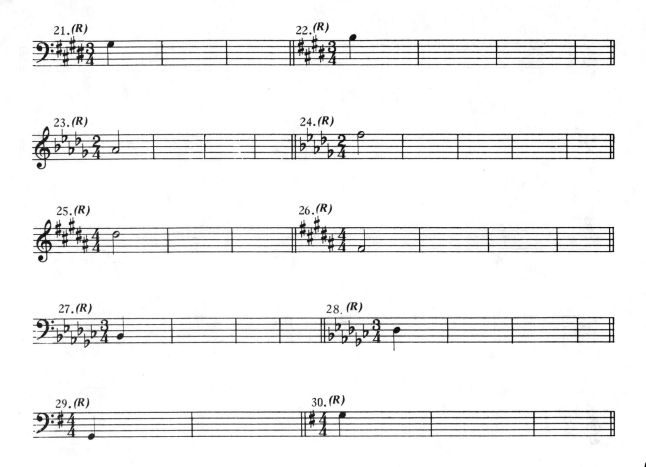

Melody 1D

Intervals: m2, M2, m3, M3

Each exercise consists of a single interval.

1. You can use your knowledge of the major and harmonic minor scale in recognizing intervals. Think of the intervals in this section as pitches of a major or harmonic minor scale:

  minor 2nd (m2) = Sounds like the **leading tone** to tonic (scale degrees 7 to 8 or ti to do) of a major scale.

  Major 2nd (M2) = Sounds like the tonic to **supertonic** (scale degrees 1 to 2 or do to re) in the major scale.

  minor 3rd (m3) = Sounds like the tonic to **mediant** (scale degrees 1 to 3 or la to do) in the minor scale.

  Major 3rd (M3) = Sounds like the tonic to mediant (scale degrees 1 to 3 or do to mi) in the major scale.

2. When you have related the sound of an **interval** to pitches found in the major or harmonic minor scale, then you are ready to write the answer.
3. Write the missing note of the interval on the staff.
4. Write the name of the interval in the space provided.

The given note is the lower of the two:

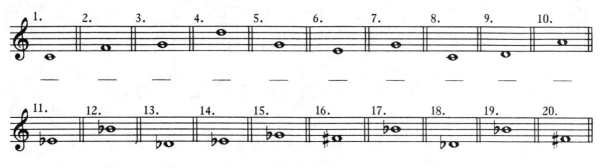

21.–40. (R)

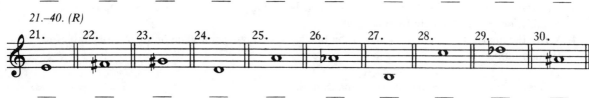

The given note is the upper of the two:

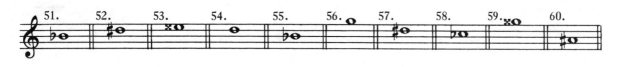

Harmony 1A

Chord Identification: I and V Triads

Each exercise consists of four **triads** in four-voice harmony.

1. Make sure you can hear the bass note of four-voice triads in root position. Outside of class play the following triads and match the pitches of the bass notes by singing them in your own voice range.

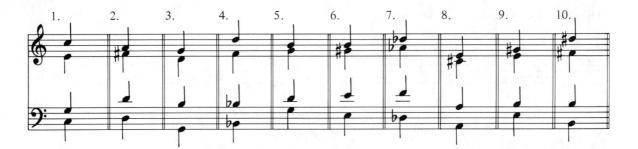

2. Listen to the four triads in each of these exercises. All are in the key of C major. Make sure you have the tonic pitch (c) well in mind.
3. All triads in numbers 1–15 are in root position. Isolate and identify the scale degree (number or syllables) of each base note by singing it.
4. Write the analysis of the four triads in the blanks by changing the scale numbers or syllables to Roman numerals.

Scale Number		Syllable		Roman Numeral
1	or	do	=	I
5	or	sol	=	V

1.–10. (R)

1. _____ _____ _____ _____   9. _____ _____ _____ _____

2. _____ _____ _____ _____   10. _____ _____ _____ _____

3. _____ _____ _____ _____   11. _____ _____ _____ _____

4. _____ _____ _____ _____   12. _____ _____ _____ _____

5. _____ _____ _____ _____   13. _____ _____ _____ _____

6. _____ _____ _____ _____   14. _____ _____ _____ _____

7. _____ _____ _____ _____   15. _____ _____ _____ _____

8. _____ _____ _____ _____

Numbers 16–25 contain **triad inversions**—the root is not the lowest note. The exercises in Harmony 1D will help you to identify inversions. Practice them before you listen to numbers 16–25.

16. _____ _____ _____ _____   21. _____ _____ _____ _____

17. _____ _____ _____ _____   22. _____ _____ _____ _____

18. _____ _____ _____ _____   23. _____ _____ _____ _____

19. _____ _____ _____ _____   24. _____ _____ _____ _____

20. _____ _____ _____ _____   25. _____ _____ _____ _____

Harmony 1B

Chord Identification:
Major and Minor Triads

Each exercise consists of a single triad. Included are both major and minor triads.

1. For numbers 1–20 (triads in simple position):
   1. Write large M for major or small m for minor in the blanks provided.
   2. If your instructor requests it, also write the triad on the staff. The roots of the triads are given.
2. For numbers 21–40 (triads in four voices—a few inversions)
   1. Circle either large M or small m indicating the sound of the triad played.
   2. Your instructor may ask you to spell the triad orally in class.

21. M m	26. M m	31. M m	36. M m
22. M m	27. M m	32. M m	37. M m
23. M m	28. M m	33. M m	38. M m
24. M m	29. M m	34. M m	39. M m
25. M m	30. M m	35. M m	40. M m

Harmony 1C

Chord Identification: Triad
Factors in the Soprano

Each exercise consists of a single **chord.** Write the number of the chord factor (1,3,5) in the soprano voice.

1. First, you will hear a triad in simple (closest possible) position. Sing it—1–3–5–3–1.
2. Then, the same triad will be played in four-part harmony. Remember that the root will be the bass note, but aside from that the chord tones in the tenor, alto, or soprano voices may be in any order.
3. After the four-voice triad is played, the soprano note will be repeated alone. Sing or *think* it immediately! Keep its pitch in your mind.
4. Recollect the sound of the simple triad first heard (No. 1 above) and determine whether the soprano pitch is the root, 3rd, or 5th. Listen again if you need to.

5. When you are convinced, write 1, 3, or 5 in the blank provided.

Write the number (1, 3, or 5) of the chord factor in the soprano.

13.–24. (R)

1. _____   7. _____   13. _____   19. _____

2. _____   8. _____   14. _____   20. _____

3. _____   9. _____   15. _____   21. _____

4. _____   10. _____   16. _____   22. _____

5. _____   11. _____   17. _____   23. _____

6. _____   12. _____   18. _____   24. _____

Harmony 1D

Chord Identification: Major and Minor Triad Positions

Each exercise consists of the three positions of the same triad in any order. Before you begin your instructor will acquaint you with the 1–3–5–3–1 pattern, which is an essential aid in identifying the triad in root position.

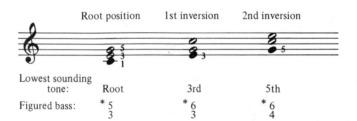

1. Listen until all three positions have been played. Locate the one in root position by relating it to the 1–3–5–3–1 pattern. Remember that 1–3–5–3–1 means that the 3rd and 5th are above the **root**—thus, **root position.**
2. When you have located the root position version write $^5_3$ in the appropriate blank (1, 2, or 3).
3. Now that you have identified the root, 3rd, and 5th, listen a second time and sing (better yet, *think*) the 3rd of the triad. When the 3rd you are singing coincides with the lowest sounding tone of an example, that example is in *first* inversion. Write $^6_3$ below it.
4. Repeat the process as described in No. 3 above but this time sing the 5th of the triad. When the 5th you are singing coincides with the lowest sounding tone of an example, that example is in *second* inversion. Write $^6_4$ below it.
5. As you become more experienced, you will discover that you can determine each position simply by listening to it as a unit—your elaborate mental calculations will become automatic!

1. _____ _____ _____   3. _____ _____ _____

2. _____ _____ _____   4. _____ _____ _____

*Indicates intervals above the lowest sounding tone

5. _____ _____ _____   13. _____ _____ _____

6. _____ _____ _____   14. _____ _____ _____

7. _____ _____ _____   15. _____ _____ _____

8. _____ _____ _____   16. _____ _____ _____

9. _____ _____ _____   17. _____ _____ _____

10. _____ _____ _____   18. _____ _____ _____
11.–20. (R)
11. _____ _____ _____   19. _____ _____ _____

12. _____ _____ _____   20. _____ _____ _____

Rhythm 1A

Rhythmic Dictation: Rhythm
Including Half-Beat Values

Each exercise consists of a two measure melody. Complete the **rhythm** (only) of each exercise on the lines provided below.

1. As you hear the preparatory measure(s) count the meter. If the meter is 4/4 count 1–2–3–4.
2. After first hearing: Say or clap the rhythm immediately.
3. After second hearing: Say meter beats and clap rhythm immediately. When you are sure of the rhythm, write it on the appropriate line.
4. If third hearing is needed: Use it to verify rhythms you have written down or to clear up any misconceptions.

If you are working with the audio tape or computer program, listen to the rhythm as many times as you require to get the right answer! Attempt to get the answer in three tries, but accuracy is the most important item for the moment.

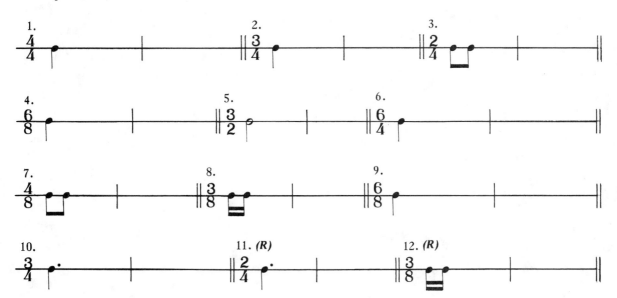

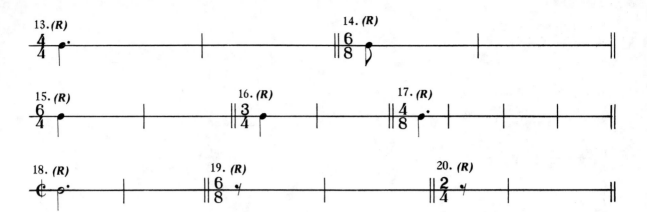

UNIT 2

Melody 2A

Scales: Scale Degrees

First you will hear a C major scale, followed by one of the pitches of that scale. Write the number (1 to 7) or syllable (do to ti) of the one pitch played.

1. Sing the scale (using numbers or syllables) until it is familiar to you.
2. If you have difficulty remembering the pitch of *all* scale degrees, be sure to remember at least 1 and 5 (do and sol). These two can be used as reference tones—landmarks that will help to locate other scale degrees.
3. When you hear the single pitch (after the scale is played) sing (or THINK) it immediately.
4. Then, relate it to one of the reference tones, tonic (first scale step) or dominant (fifth scale step)— whichever is closest, and sing stepwise to that reference tone.
5. You will know the identity of the pitch played by the number of scale steps you sang to get to the reference tone, tones around which other scale tones may be located.
6. When you are sure of your answer, write it in the appropriate blank.

1. _____
2. _____
3. _____
4. _____
5. _____
6. _____
7. _____
8. _____
9. _____
10. _____

11. _____
12. _____
13. _____
14. _____
15. _____
16. _____
17. _____
18. _____
19. _____
20. _____

Melody 2B

Melodic Dictation: Dictation
Employing m2, M2, m3, M3

Each exercise consists of a short melody.

1. Memorize the melody before trying to write it down.
2. If your instructor requests, sing the entire melody using solfeggio syllables (do re mi) or numbers (1, 2, 3, and so on).

3. When you know the melody thoroughly, write it on the appropriate staff.

*(R) means recorded.

Melody 2C

Mode Identification: Dorian, Phrygian, Lydian, and Mixolydian Modes

Each exercise consists of the Dorian, Phrygian, Lydian, or Mixolydian scale.

DORIAN MODE is the same as the natural minor scale with a raised 6th. Listen for a natural minor scale with a *raised 6th degree*.

PHRYGIAN MODE is the same as the natural minor except for a lowered 2nd. Listen for a natural minor scale with a *lowered 2nd degree*.

LYDIAN MODE is the same as the major scale except for a raised 4th. Listen for a major scale with a *raised 4th degree*.

MIXOLYDIAN MODE is the same as the major scale except for a lowered 7th. Listen for a major scale with a *lowered 7th degree*.

In the blanks provided, name the mode you hear.

1. _____   6. _____
2. _____   7. _____
3. _____   8. _____
4. _____   9. _____
5. _____   10. _____

In numbers 11–20 the modal scales will be played in reverse order—from the highest tone to the lowest.

11. _____   13. _____
12. _____   14. _____
15. _____   18. _____
16. _____   19. _____
17. _____   20. _____

Melody 2D

New Intervals: P5 and P4

Intervals studied to date: m2, M2, m3, M3,
Each exercise consists of a single interval. The first note is given.

1. Write the second note of the interval on the staff.
2. Place the name of the interval (P4, m2, M3, and so on) in the blank provided.
3. To help you recognize intervals think of them as parts of a scale:

   P5   =   Tonic to 5th of a major or minor scale.

   P4   =   Tonic to 4th scale degree of a major or minor scale.

   M3   =   Tonic to 3rd of a major scale.

   m3   =   Tonic to 3rd of a minor scale.

   M2   =   Tonic to 2nd degree of a major or minor scale.

   m2   =   Leading to tonic of a major or harmonic minor scale.

The second note is above the given tone:

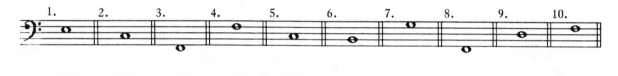

11.–20. (R)

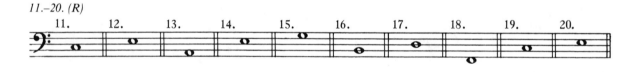

The second note is below the given tone:

Harmony 2A

Chord Identification: I, IV, and V Triads

Each exercise consists of four chords in four-part block harmony. Write the Roman numeral analysis of each chord in the blanks provided.

A list of suggested strategies for this section can be found in Harmony 1A.

Numbers 1–15 consist of the following root-position triads only:

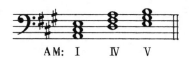

AM: I   IV   V

1.–10. (R)

1. _____ _____ _____ _____   9. _____ _____ _____ _____

2. _____ _____ _____ _____   10. _____ _____ _____ _____

3. _____ _____ _____ _____   11. _____ _____ _____ _____

4. _____ _____ _____ _____   12. _____ _____ _____ _____

5. _____ _____ _____ _____   13. _____ _____ _____ _____

6. _____ _____ _____ _____   14. _____ _____ _____ _____

7. _____ _____ _____ _____   15. _____ _____ _____ _____

8. _____ _____ _____ _____

Numbers 16–25 contain at least one inversion:

16. _____ _____ _____ _____   18. _____ _____ _____ _____

17. _____ _____ _____ _____   19. _____ _____ _____ _____

Harmony 2B

Chord Identification: Major, Minor, and Diminished Triads

Each exercise consists of a single triad. Included are diminished half step lower than Perfect, major, or minor intervals as well as major and minor triads.

1. For numbers 1–10 (triads in simple position):
    1. Write large M for major, small m for minor, and small d for diminished triads in the blanks provided.
    2. If your instructor requests it, also write the triad on the staff. The ROOTS of the triads are given.
2. For numbers 11–30 (triads in four voices—a few inversions)
    1. Write large M, small m, or small d in the blanks provided.
    2. Your instructor may ask you to spell the triad orally in class.

11. _____	21. _____
12. _____	22. _____
13. _____	23. _____
14. _____	24. _____
15. _____	25. _____
16. _____	26. _____
17. _____	27. _____
18. _____	28. _____
19. _____	29. _____
20. _____	30. _____

Harmony 2C

Chord Identification: Triad Positions

Each exercise is a single triad in four-part harmony. Indicate the triad position. Your answers should be:

Root Position   = $\frac{5}{3}$

First Inversion   = $\frac{6}{3}$

Second Inversion = $\frac{6}{4}$

The techniques in Harmony 1D will help you.

Example:

1. _____   11. _____

2. _____   12. _____

3. _____   13. _____

4. _____   14. _____

5. _____   15. _____

6. _____   16. _____

7. _____   17. _____

8. _____   18. _____

9. _____   19. _____

10. _____   20. _____

Harmony 2D

Dictation: The I, IV, and V Triads in Four-Part Harmonic Phrases

Each exercise consists of a phrase containing seven chords in root position.

1. Listen to the phrase. In this assignment the first triad is always the tonic and all triads are in root position.
2. Sing as you listen, matching pitches with the bass notes.
3. With as few listenings as possible, memorize the succession of bass notes. To test yourself, sing them without listening to the phrase.
4. Begin associating solfeggio syllables or scale numbers with the pitches. Remember, in this assignment the first bass note is always the tonic. Gradually you will develop skill in relating each pitch to a specific syllable or number.
5. Convert the syllables or numbers to actual pitches—do fa sol (or 1 4 5) in the key of C means the notes C F G.

6. When the conversion process is complete, write the pitches on the **bass clef** staff in notation (remember, stems *DOWN*).
7. Since all of the triads in this assignment are in root position, you can also write the Roman numeral analysis in the blanks below the staves.
8. If your instructor requests, repeat the process with the three remaining voices (soprano, alto, and tenor).
9. If your instructor asks you to write out all four voices, you can check your choices by comparing them with the Roman numeral analysis. Do the notes in all four voices match the triad analysis you selected earlier?

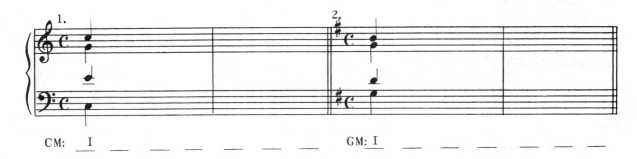

CM: I _ _ _ _ _ _   GM: I _ _ _ _ _ _

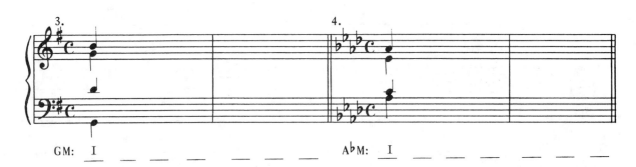

GM: I _ _ _ _ _ _   A♭M: I _ _ _ _ _ _

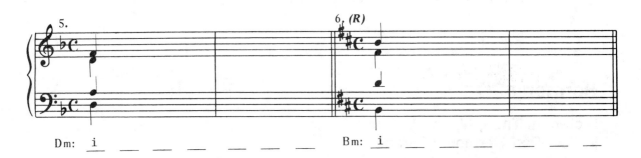

Dm: i _ _ _ _ _ _   Bm: i _ _ _ _ _ _

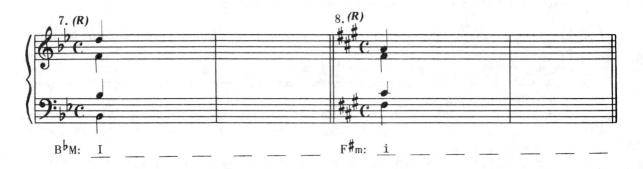

B♭M: I _ _ _ _ _ _   F♯m: i _ _ _ _ _ _

Harmony 2E

Nonharmonic Tones: Introduction

Each exercise consists of a **nonharmonic** tone in a two-voice setting. Write the name of the nonharmonic tone in the appropriate blank.

1. Nonharmonic tones played in this section are:
   Unaccented passing tone
   Unaccented neighboring tone
   Escape tone
   Anticipation
   Accented passing tone
   Accented neighboring tone
   Suspension (9–8, 7–6, 4–3, 2–3)
2. Definitions of the nonharmonic tones played in this section are available in the Glossary, or consult your theory text.
3. A sound pattern is a three note series of pitches, with the nonharmonic tone in the middle. The *sound pattern* of each nonharmonic tone is especially helpful in ear training.
4. Some items that are common to all of the above listed nonharmonic tones:
   a. The nonharmonic tone is always *dissonant* (9th, 7th, 4th, 2nd).
   b. The nonharmonic tone is always the *middle* note of the pattern.
   c. The two notes on either side are always *consonant*.
5. One nonharmonic tone can be distinguished from another by the pattern of movement—by (S)tep, by (L)eap, or by (R)epeated pitch. The pattern of movement helps to distinguish among all of the above listed nonharmonic tones except the passing tone and the neighboring tone.
6. Passing tones and neighboring tones can be distinguished only by the direction of the movement—

   passing tone   = down-down or up-up

   neighboring tone = up down or down-up

7. The following example illustrates nonharmonic tones in a one-voice setting. Note that in all instances (1) the nonharmonic tone is dissonant, (2) the nonharmonic tone is the middle note, and (3) the first and third notes are consonant.

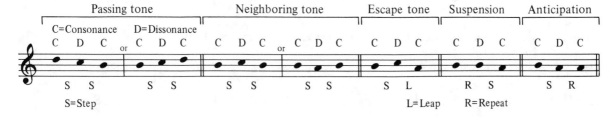

8. Practice playing these patterns until you know them thoroughly.
9. Before playing the two-voice illustrations, your instructor will play randomly some of the one-voice examples to help acquaint you with the distinguishing characteristics of each nonharmonic tone type.

Examples:

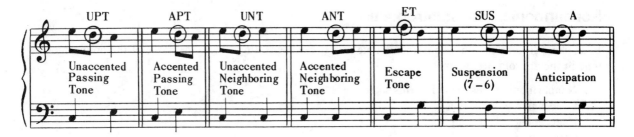

Circle the correct nonharmonic tone abbreviation:

Nonharmonic tones are in the upper voice in numbers 1–10:

1. UPT APT UNT ANT ET SUS A   6. UPT APT UNT ANT ET SUS A

2. UPT APT UNT ANT ET SUS A   7. UPT APT UNT ANT ET SUS A

3. UPT APT UNT ANT ET SUS A   8. UPT APT UNT ANT ET SUS A

4. UPT APT UNT ANT ET SUS A   9. UPT APT UNT ANT ET SUS A

5. UPT APT UNT ANT ET SUS A   10. UPT APT UNT ANT ET SUS A

Nonharmonic tones are in the lower voice in number 11–20:

11. UPT APT UNT ANT ET SUS A   16. UPT APT UNT ANT ET SUS A

12. UPT APT UNT ANT ET SUS A   17. UPT APT UNT ANT ET SUS A

13. UPT APT UNT ANT ET SUS A   18. UPT APT UNT ANT ET SUS A

14. UPT APT UNT ANT ET SUS A   19. UPT APT UNT ANT ET SUS A

15. UPT APT UNT ANT ET SUS A   20. UPT APT UNT ANT ET SUS A

Nonharmonic tones may be in either upper or lower voice in numbers 21–30:

21. UPT APT UNT ANT ET SUS A   26. UPT APT UNT ANT ET SUS A

22. UPT APT UNT ANT ET SUS A   27. UPT APT UNT ANT ET SUS A

23. UPT APT UNT ANT ET SUS A   28. UPT APT UNT ANT ET SUS A

24. UPT APT UNT ANT ET SUS A   29. UPT APT UNT ANT ET SUS A

25. UPT APT UNT ANT ET SUS A   30. UPT APT UNT ANT ET SUS A

Harmony 2F

Error Detection: Triads with Errors

Each exercise consists of a single triad. The first five examples are triads in root position, and the remaining five are first inversions (bass note is the third of the triad).

As played by the instructor, one of the four voices contains an error in pitch.

Indicate the voice containing the error:

S = Soprano   A = Alto   T = Tenor (no errors in the bass)

1. Play each exercise on a piano with the damper pedal depressed. Try to match by singing the pitch of each voice (soprano, alto, tenor, and bass). Use an octave substitution for those voices out of your range.
2. When you can do this with accuracy, try the exercises below.
3. In class match the pitches of the voices by *imagining* rather than actually singing the pitches.
4. Reconstructing sounds in your mind is called tonal imagery, and mastering this trick is one of the most important skills you will acquire in an ear training course!

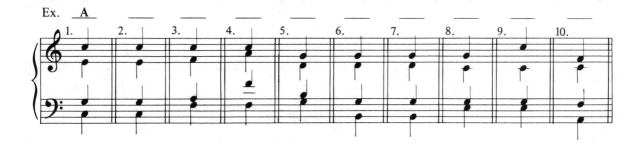

Rhythm 2A

Rhythmic Dictation: Duple and Triple Subdivisions of the Beat

Each exercise consists of a three-measure melody. Complete the rhythm only of each exercise on the lines provided.

1. As you hear the preparatory measure(s) count the meter. If the meter is 3/4 count 1–2–3.
2. After first hearing: Say or clap the rhythm immediately.
3. After second hearing: Count the meter beats and clap rhythm immediately. When you are sure of the rhythm, write it on the appropriate line.
4. If third hearing is needed: Use it to verify rhythms you have written down or to clear up any misconceptions.

Listen to the rhythm as many times as you require to get the right answer. Accuracy is the most important item for the moment.

The example indicates the correct procedure.

UNIT 3

Melody 3A

Scales: Scale Degrees

1. The instructor first plays a scale, then two tones of that scale.
2. Identify the two scale degrees played. The instructor will tell you whether to use scale numbers or syllables.
3. Review Melody 2A.

Instructor plays:

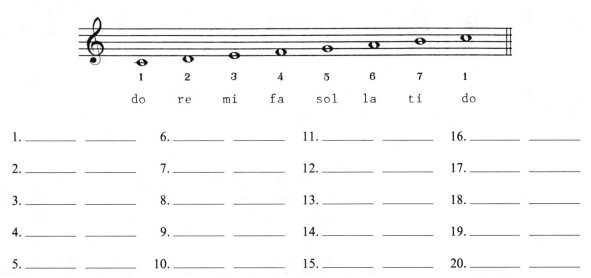

1. _____ _____   6. _____ _____   11. _____ _____   16. _____ _____

2. _____ _____   7. _____ _____   12. _____ _____   17. _____ _____

3. _____ _____   8. _____ _____   13. _____ _____   18. _____ _____

4. _____ _____   9. _____ _____   14. _____ _____   19. _____ _____

5. _____ _____   10. _____ _____   15. _____ _____   20. _____ _____

Melody 3B

Melodic Dictation: Using m2, M2, m3, M3, P4, P5

Each exercise consists of a short melody that begins on the tonic pitch.

1. Memorize the melody before trying to write it down.
2. If your instructor requests, sing the entire melody using solfeggio syllables or numbers. Keep trying to replace singing out loud with *thinking*—imagining the melody in your mind.
3. When you know the melody thoroughly, write it on the appropriate staff.

*(R) means recorded.

Melody 3C

Melodic Figure Identification: Sequences and Rhythmic Repetition

Each exercise consists of a melodic excerpt from music literature that contains a sequence or a rhythmic repetition.

SEQUENCE   The immediate restating of a melodic figure at a higher or lower pitch so that the structure of the figure is maintained. Each unit is called a segment.

Tchaikovsky: *Symphony no. 6*

RHYTHMIC REPETITION   The rhythm of a significant portion of the excerpt is repeated. The pitches (at least a majority) are not repeated.

Weber: *Jubel Ouvertüre*

Listen carefully to each melody as played and circle:

SEQUENCE—   when you hear a sequence
RHYTHMIC REPETITION—   when you hear a rhythm repeated but no melodic
                            sequence
NEITHER—   when you hear neither a sequence nor a repeated
                            rhythm

1. SEQ.	RHY. REP.	NEITHER		8. SEQ.	RHY. REP.	NEITHER
2. SEQ.	RHY. REP.	NEITHER		9. SEQ.	RHY. REP.	NEITHER
3. SEQ.	RHY. REP.	NEITHER		10. SEQ.	RHY. REP.	NEITHER
4. SEQ.	RHY. REP.	NEITHER		11. SEQ.	RHY. REP.	NEITHER
5. SEQ.	RHY. REP.	NEITHER		12. SEQ.	RHY. REP.	NEITHER
6. SEQ.	RHY. REP.	NEITHER		13. SEQ.	RHY. REP.	NEITHER
7. SEQ.	RHY. REP.	NEITHER		14. SEQ.	RHY. REP.	NEITHER

Melody 3D

Scales: Major Scale and Three Forms of the Minor Scale

Exercises 1–10   consist of a major, natural minor, harmonic minor, or melodic minor scale.

Exercises 11–20   consist of short melodic excerpts from music literature based on one of these scales.

Natural minor   follows the key signature.

Harmonic minor   key signature plus raised 7th degree.

Ascending melodic minor   key signature plus raised 6th and 7th degrees.

Major   follows the key signature.

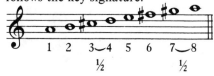

Write the name of the scale in the blank provided.

1. _____   9. _____

2. _____   10. _____

3. _____   (R)11. _____

4. _____   (R)12. _____

5. _____   (R)13. _____

6. _____   (R)14. _____

7. _____   (R)15. _____

8. _____   (R)16. _____

(R)17. _____   (R)19. _____

(R)18. _____   (R)20. _____

Melody 3E

Interval Review: Intervals Studied to Date—m2, M2, m3, M3, P4, P5

Each exercise consists of a single interval. The first note is given.

1. Write the second note of the interval on the staff.
2. Place the name of the interval (P4, m2, M3, etc.) in the blank provided.
3. To help you recognize intervals think of them as parts of a scale or triad:

   P5 = Tonic to 5th of a major or minor scale.

   P4 = Tonic to 4th scale degree of a major or minor scale.

   M3 = Tonic to 3rd of a major scale.

   m3 = Tonic to 3rd of a minor triad.

   M2 = Tonic to 2nd degree of a major or minor scale.

   m2 = Leading to tonic of a major or harmonic minor scale.

4. In numbers 31 through 60, singing through the interval (think of the first pitch as tonic, and sing the successive scale degrees to the second pitch) should still be practiced. For instance, if the interval is from C down to G, sing scale degrees 8 (or 1, 7, 6, 5.)
5. When you get to 5 you will notice that this pitch matches the second pitch played, and you will know that it is a P4th.
6. Remember that when singing *down,* intervals are inverted, so 5 (going up) means 4 (going down).
7. When practicing for the first time, forget about inversions and count (on your fingers) the number of scale steps you descend to match the second pitch. Later, when you have had considerable practice, experience will help you to recognize all intervals without needing to count.

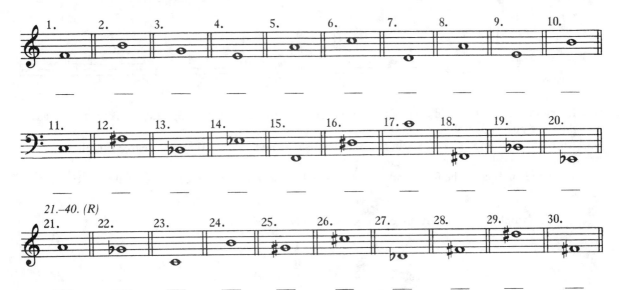

The given note is the upper note of the interval:

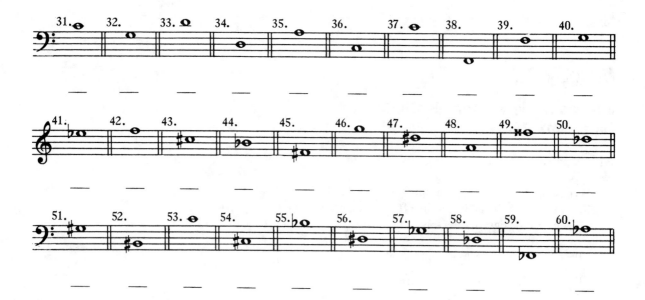

Harmony 3A

Chord Identification: I, ii, and V Triads

Each exercise consists of four triads in four-voice harmony.

1. Make sure you can hear the bass note of four-voice triads in root position. Outside of class play the following triads and try to match the pitches of the bass notes by singing them in your own voice range.

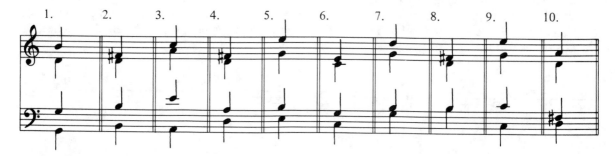

2. Listen to the four triads in each of these exercises. All are in the key of G major. Make sure you have the tonic pitch (G) well in mind.
3. All triads in Numbers 1–15 are in root position, isolate and identify the scale degree (number or syllable) of each bass note by singing it.
4. Write the analysis of the four triads in the blanks by changing the numbers or syllables to Roman numerals.

Scale Number		Syllable		Roman Numeral
1	or	do	=	I
2	or	re	=	ii
5	or	sol	=	V

5. Numbers 16–25 contain triad inversions.

Numbers 1–15 contain root-position triads only:

1. _____ _____ _____ _____   (R) 9. _____ _____ _____ _____

2. _____ _____ _____ _____   (R)10. _____ _____ _____ _____

3. _____ _____ _____ _____   (R)11. _____ _____ _____ _____

4. _____ _____ _____ _____   (R)12. _____ _____ _____ _____

5. _____ _____ _____ _____   (R)13. _____ _____ _____ _____

6. _____ _____ _____ _____   (R)14. _____ _____ _____ _____

7. _____ _____ _____ _____   (R)15. _____ _____ _____ _____

(R)8. _____ _____ _____ _____

Numbers 16–25 contain inversions:

16. _____ _____ _____ _____   21. _____ _____ _____ _____

17. _____ _____ _____ _____   22. _____ _____ _____ _____

18. _____ _____ _____ _____   23. _____ _____ _____ _____

19. _____ _____ _____ _____   24. _____ _____ _____ _____

20. _____ _____ _____ _____   25. _____ _____ _____ _____

Harmony 3B

Harmonic Dictation: I, ii, IV, and V
Triads in Four-Part Chorale Phrases

Each exercise consists of a phrase from a chorale. Numbers 7–14 were harmonized by Bach.

1.	Numbers	Harmonic Vocabulary	Triad Positions	Nonharmonic Tones
	1–6	I or i, ii, V	All root position	UPT and 4–3 SUS only
	7–9	I and V only	Root position and 1st inversion	UPT, APT, and 2–3 SUS
	10–14	I, IV, and V only	Root position, 1st inversion, 2nd inversion	UPT, LNT, and 4–3 SUS
	15–16	I, ii, IV, and V	Root position, and 1st inversion	UPT only

2. Indicate the Roman numeral analysis of each triad in the blanks provided.
3. List nonharmonic tones beneath the harmonic analysis.
4. If the instructor requests it, give the melodic line of both the soprano and bass voices.
5. If the instructor requests it, give the melodic line of both the alto and tenor voices.

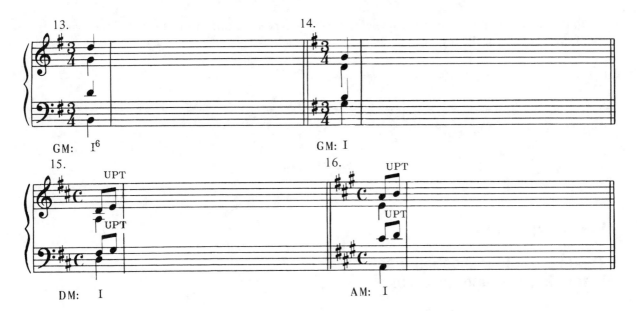

Harmony 3C

Cadence Identification: Cadence Types

Each exercise consists of four chords in four-part harmony. The final two chords represent one of the traditional cadence types.

1. The cadence types:

PERFECT AUTHENTIC   V to I with both chords in root-position. The tonic is the soprano note in the I chord.

IMPERFECT AUTHENTIC   V to I or vii°⁶ to I with at least one of the following circumstances present:
(a) the V may be in inversion
(b) the final soprano note is *not* the tonic

HALF   I, ii, or IV proceeding to V. The first chord of the two may be in inversion.

PLAGAL   IV to I

DECEPTIVE   In these exercises: V to vi (or VI)

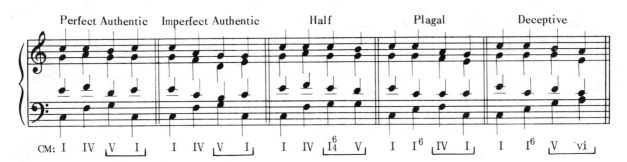

2. In the blanks provided, write the name of the cadence type you hear. The first chord of the four is always the tonic of the key.

1. _____   5. _____   9. _____   13. _____

2. _____   6. _____   10. _____   14. _____

3. _____   7. _____   11. _____   15. _____

4. _____   8. _____   12. _____   16. _____

Harmony 3D

Triad Factor Identification: Factors in the Soprano and Bass Voice

Each exercise consists of a single triad played in four-part harmony.

1. Indicate the chord factor (1–3–5) in the soprano voice.
2. Indicate the chord factor (1–3–5) in the bass voice.

SOPRANO FACTOR	BASS FACTOR	SOPRANO FACTOR	BASS FACTOR	SOPRANO FACTOR	BASS FACTOR	SOPRANO FACTOR	BASS FACTOR
				11.–20. (R)			
1. _____ _____		6. _____ _____		11. _____ _____		16. _____ _____	
2. _____ _____		7. _____ _____		12. _____ _____		17. _____ _____	
3. _____ _____		8. _____ _____		13. _____ _____		18. _____ _____	
4. _____ _____		9. _____ _____		14. _____ _____		19. _____ _____	
5. _____ _____		10. _____ _____		15. _____ _____		20. _____ _____	

Harmony 3E

Nonharmonic Tones: Nonharmonic Tones in a Two-Voice Setting

Each exercise consists of a nonharmonic tone in a two voice setting. Write the name of the nonharmonic tone in the appropriate blank.

1. Nonharmonic tones played in numbers 1 through 10:

Unaccented passing tone   **Accented passing tone**
Unaccented neighboring tone   **Accented neighboring tone**
Escape tone   **Suspension (9–8, 7–6, 4–3, 2–3)**
Anticipation

2. Review Harmony 2E.

3. Write the name of the nonharmonic tones in the appropriate blanks:

1. _____   6. _____

2. _____   7. _____

3. _____   8. _____

4. _____   9. _____

5. _____   10. _____

4. Nonharmonic tones presented in numbers 11–20:
   Appoggiatura   **Retardation**
   Pedal Point (or Pedal Tone)   **Changing Tones**

5. Observe the additional sound patterns provided by the **appoggiatura, retardation, pedal point,** and **changing tones:**

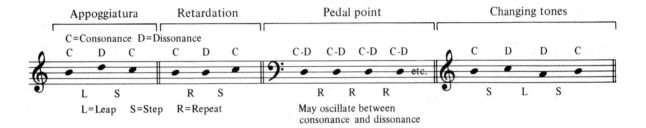

6. Only the appoggiatura and retardation are three-note patterns. Changing tones usually consist of a four-note pattern distinguished by two dissonances, and the pedal point may be of any length. For a more detailed description of the four nonharmonic tones listed, see the Glossary, your theory text, or the *Harvard Dictionary of Music.*

7. The following are nonharmonic tone examples in a two-voice setting:

8. Numbers 11–20 includes any of the 11 nonharmonic tone types studied. Write the name of the nonharmonic tone in the appropriate blank:

11. _____   14. _____

12. _____   15. _____

13. _____   *(R)*16. _____

9. Numbers 21–30 are examples of nonharmonic tones in a four-voice setting. Write the names of the nonharmonic tones in the appropriate blanks:

21. _____ 26. _____

22. _____ 27. _____

23. _____ 28. _____

24. _____ 29. _____

25. _____ 30. _____

Rhythm 3A

Error Detection

1. Each exercise consists of six or eight measures of music, and contains errors in two measures (the notation does not correspond with what is played).
2. Before listening to each excerpt, clap, say, or *think* it through from beginning to end. Make sure that you know what the exercise sounds like as written.
3. Circle the measure number where the notation is different from that played by the instructor.

Rhythm 3B

Rhythmic Dictation: Rhythmic Figures
Including Half-Beat Values

Each exercise consists of two measures of 2/4, 3/4, or 4/4 meter.

1. For numbers 1–10, the meter signature and first-note value(s) are given.
2. For numbers 11–20, nothing is given, but the instructor will provide the basic beat before beginning the exercise.
3. For helpful suggestions see Rhythm 1A.
4. Complete the rhythm using a neutral pitch:

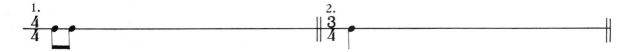

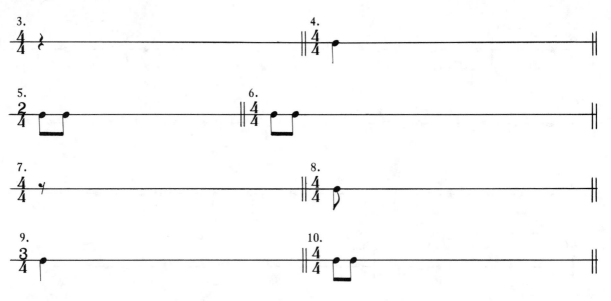

5. Write the meter signature and the rhythm using a neutral pitch. The instructor will provide the meter beat before beginning each exercise.

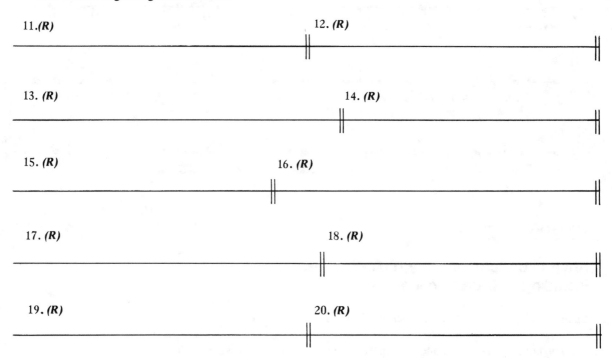

UNIT 4

Melody 4A

Melodic Dictation: Scalewise Passages and Arpeggiations of I and V

Each exercise consists of a short melodic phrase. Complete the phrase on the staff in notation.

1. As you listen to each melody the first time, try to memorize it immediately in its entirety.
2. Do *not* try to write anything on paper yet! You will learn almost nothing by trying to write too early.
3. Before you hear the melody a second time, sing as much of it (from first hearing) as you can.
4. A second or third hearing should provide the pitches you missed, so you are probably able to sing the entire melody from memory now.
5. Listen as many times as you need to in order to memorize the entire melody.
6. Only after you have the entire melody memorized should you attempt to write anything on paper!
7. Observe that when you have the melody memorized, you can slow it down sufficiently to write the notes on the staff as you sing (or preferably *think*).
8. Write the melody on the staff in music notation.

Complete each melody on the staff in notation.

*(R) means recorded.

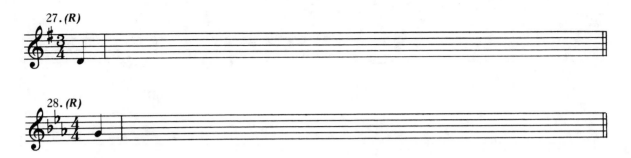

Melody 4B

Error Detection: Melodies with Errors

Each exercise consists of a short melody with *three* errors in pitch.

1. Review Melody 1B.
2. Circle the numbers representing the tones that are different from those played by the instructor.

Melody 4C

Melodic Figure Identification

Each exercise consists of a short melodic excerpt containing a sequence, a false sequence, or a rhythmic interruption.

Indicate which of the following devices is contained in each excerpt.

SEQUENCE   The immediate restating of a melodic figure at a higher or lower pitch
                             so that the structure of the figure is maintained.

FALSE SEQUENCE   The figure is partially repeated and partially sequenced.

RHYTHMIC REPETITION   The rhythm is repeated, but the pitches are not sequenced or
                             repeated.

Listen carefully to each melody as played; circle the device contained in the excerpt.

1. SEQUENCE   (when you hear a sequence)
2. FALSE SEQUENCE   (when you hear a false sequence)
3. RHYTHMIC REPETITION   (when you hear a rhythm repeated but no melodic sequence)
4. NONE   (when you hear none of the three devices listed above)

1.	Sequence	False sequence	Rhythmic repetition	None
2.	Sequence	False sequence	Rhythmic repetition	None
3.	Sequence	False sequence	Rhythmic repetition	None
(R) 4.	Sequence	False sequence	Rhythmic repetition	None
(R) 5.	Sequence	False sequence	Rhythmic repetition	None
(R) 6.	Sequence	False sequence	Rhythmic repetition	None
(R) 7.	Sequence	False sequence	Rhythmic repetition	None
8.	Sequence	False sequence	Rhythmic repetition	None
9.	Sequence	False sequence	Rhythmic repetition	None
10.	Sequence	False sequence	Rhythmic repetition	None
11.	Sequence	False sequence	Rhythmic repetition	None
12.	Sequence	False sequence	Rhythmic repetition	None

Melody 4D

Intervals: m6 and M6

Intervals studied to date: m2, M2, m3, M3, P4, P5

Each exercise consists of a single interval. The first note is given.

1. Write the second note of the interval on the staff.
2. Place the name of the interval (P4, m6, M6, and so on) in the blank provided.
3. To help you recognize the new intervals think of them as parts of a scale:

Second note ABOVE the first: M6 = Tonic to 6th of a major scale

Second note BELOW the first: M6 = When you hear the second pitch, think of it as the tonic of a major scale.

Second note above the first: m6 = Tonic to 6th of a minor scale.

Second note below the first: m6 = When you hear the second pitch, think of it as the tonic of a minor scale.

The given note is the lower of the two:

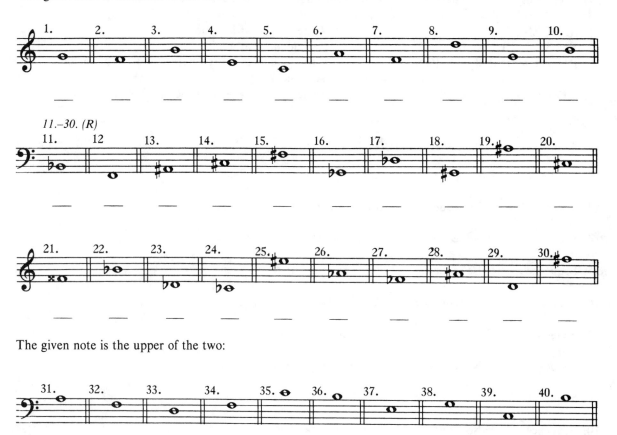

The given note is the upper of the two:

Harmony 4A

Chord Identification: Distinguishing among the I, ii, IV, and V Triads

Each exercise consists of a harmonic progression of four chords in four-part harmony. The harmonies are limited to the I, ii, IV, and V triads.

1. Write the Roman numeral analysis of the triads in the blanks provided.
2. Unless the instructor requests it, do not indicate inversions.
3. The example indicates the correct procedure.

EXAMPLE:

The instructor plays the following:

DM: I   ii   V   I

Response:

Ex. ___I___ ___ii___ ___IV___ ___V___

Numbers1–15 contain root-position triads only.

(R)1. _____ _____ _____ _____   (R) 9. _____ _____ _____ _____

(R)2. _____ _____ _____ _____   (R)10. _____ _____ _____ _____

(R)3. _____ _____ _____ _____   11. _____ _____ _____ _____

(R)4. _____ _____ _____ _____   12. _____ _____ _____ _____

(R)5. _____ _____ _____ _____   13. _____ _____ _____ _____

(R)6. _____ _____ _____ _____   14. _____ _____ _____ _____

(R)7. _____ _____ _____ _____   15. _____ _____ _____ _____

(R)8. _____ _____ _____ _____

Numbers 16–25 contain inversions.

16. _____ _____ _____ _____   21. _____ _____ _____ _____

17. _____ _____ _____ _____   22. _____ _____ _____ _____

18. _____ _____ _____ _____   23. _____ _____ _____ _____

19. _____ _____ _____ _____   24. _____ _____ _____ _____

20. _____ _____ _____ _____   25. _____ _____ _____ _____

Harmony 4B

Harmonic Rhythm

Each exercise consists of a short excerpt of music.

1. In this section you will apply your listening experiences to a composition from the literature of music. The strategy is simple to explain but often difficult to put in practice—place an "X" at each point in the music when you hear most (or any) chord factors change enough to form a different harmony.
2. In the first five examples you can follow the melody and note possible changes simply by assessing the melodic pitches.
3. The remaining five excerpts require concentration on the quality and makeup of each harmony.
4. This is your first opportunity to listen especially for harmonic rhythm; do not be discouraged if you make a few mistakes. Review each error carefully, and try to determine what confused you.
5. If you are working outside of class, and make a number of errors, play the exercise several times *after* answering. Assessing the cause of a mistake is the best way to avoid similar errors later on.
6. Place an "X" at each point in the melody where the harmony changes. The example indicates the correct procedure.

Example:

7. In the following exercises, the melody is replaced by melodic rhythm only.
   Circle the numbers that represent chord changes.
   If a chord change occurs at another point, place the circle between the numbers.

6.

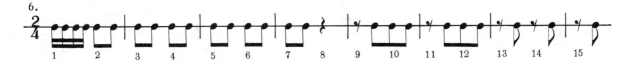

7.

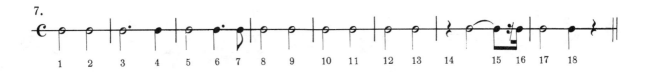

8.

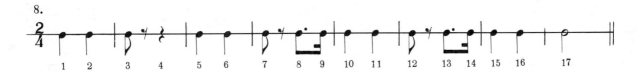

9.

10.

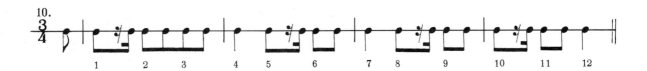

Harmony 4C

Harmonic Dictation: I, ii, IV, and V
Triads in Four-Part Chorale Phrases

Each exercise consists of a phrase from a **chorale.** Numbers 7 through 16 were harmonized by Bach. The harmonic vocabulary is as follows:

Numbers 1–6:	All triads are in root position.
Numbers 7–16:	Triads are in inversion as well as root position.

1. Indicate the Roman numeral analysis of each triad in the blanks provided.
2. List any nonharmonic tones beneath the harmonic analysis.
3. If the instructor requests it, give the melodic line of both the soprano and bass voices.
4. If the instructor requests it, give the melodic line of both the alto and tenor voices.

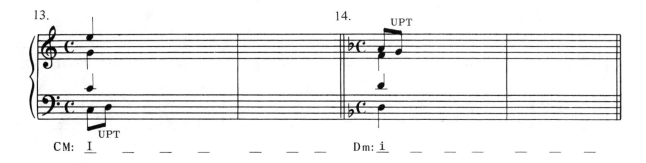

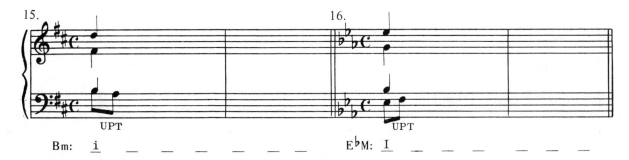

Harmony 4D

Chord Identification: Writing Major, Minor, Diminished, and Augmented Triads

Each exercise consists of a single triad in four-part harmony. Each triad shown is correct except for the accidentals.

1. Write the type of triad (major, minor, diminished, augmented) in the blank below the staves.
2. Write the accidentals necessary to correct each triad.

The bass note is *always* correct.

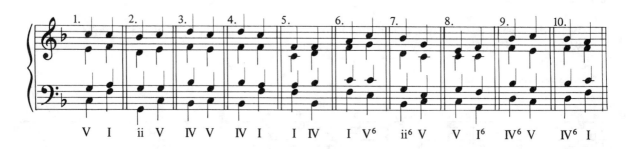

Harmony 4E

Error Detection: Triads

Each exercise consists of two triads in four parts.

1. As played by the instructor, one note in each exercise is incorrect. The bass voice contains no errors.
2. Indicate the chord (no. 1 or no. 2) containing the error.
3. Indicate which voice contains the error:

     S = Soprano   A = Alto   T = Tenor

The example indicates the correct procedure.

Ex.
Chord: 2   ____   ____   ____   ____   ____   ____   ____   ____   ____   ____

Voice: T   ____   ____   ____   ____   ____   ____   ____   ____   ____   ____

Rhythm 4A

Error Detection: Half-Beat Values

Each exercise consists of a phrase of music. On one beat, the rhythm will be different from that played by the instructor.

Circle the number representing the beat that is changed.

Rhythm 4B

Rhythmic Dictation: Half-Beat
Values in Syncopation

Each exercise consists of a phrase of music.

Complete the rhythm (neutral pitch) on the staff in notation.

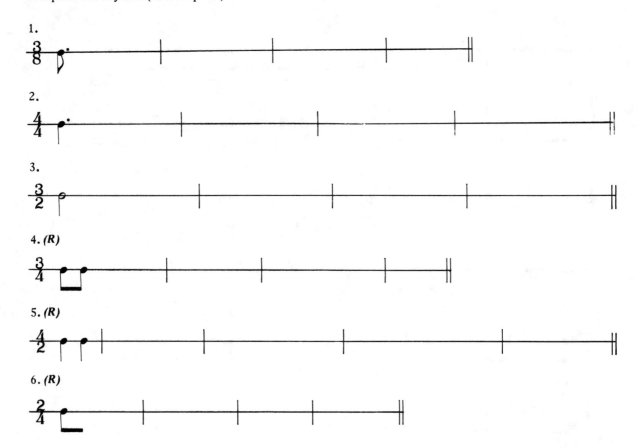

UNIT 5

Melody 5A

Melodic Dictation: Melodies Outlining the I, IV, V (and vii°⁶) Triads

Each exercise consists of a short melody.

Complete the composition on the staff in notation.

*(R) means recorded.

Melody 5B

Error Detection: Errors in Melodies
Outlining the I, IV, and V Triads

Each exercise consists of a melody containing an error or errors in pitch.

1. Melodies 1–20 contain one error in pitch.
2. Melodies 21–25 contain three errors in pitch.
3. Circle each number representing the tone that is different from the one played.

Each melody contains THREE errors:

21. (R)

1 2 3 4 5 6 7 8 9 10 11 12 13 14 15 16 17 18 19 20

22. (R)

1 2 3 4 5 6 7 8 9 10 11 12

23. (R)

1 2 3 4 5 6 7 8 9 10 11 12 13 14 15 16 17 18 19 20 21 22 23

24. (R)

1 2 3 4 5 6 7 8 9 10 11 12 13 14 15

25. (R)

1 2 3 4 5 6 7 8 9 10 11 12 13 14 15 16

Melody 5C

Scales: Identifying Scale Degrees

1. The instructor first plays a scale, then three tones of that scale.
2. Identify the three scale degrees played. The instructor will tell you whether to use scale numbers or syllables.
3. The instructor plays:

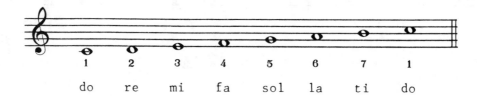

1 2 3 4 5 6 7 1

do re mi fa sol la ti do

These tones are in ascending order:

1. _____ _____ _____

2. _____ _____ _____

3. _____ _____ _____

4. _____ _____ _____

5. _____ _____ _____

6. _____ _____ _____

7. _____ _____ _____

8. _____ _____ _____

9. _____ _____ _____

10. _____ _____ _____

11. _____ _____ _____

12. _____ _____ _____

13. _____ _____ _____

14. _____ _____ _____

15. _____ _____ _____

16. _____ _____ _____

These tones are in mixed ascending order:

17. _____ _____ _____

18. _____ _____ _____

19. _____ _____ _____

20. _____ _____ _____

21. _____ _____ _____

22. _____ _____ _____

23. _____ _____ _____

24. _____ _____ _____

25. _____ _____ _____

26. _____ _____ _____

27. _____ _____ _____

28. _____ _____ _____

29. _____ _____ _____

30. _____ _____ _____

31. _____ _____ _____

32. _____ _____ _____

Melody 5D

Intervals: The Tritone

Intervals studied to date: m2, M2, m3, M3, P4, P5, m6, M6

Each exercise consists of a single interval. The first note is given.

1. Write the second note of the interval on the staff.
2. Place the name of the interval in the blank provided.
3. The **tritone** (augmented 4th and diminished 5th) occurs in both major and harmonic minor from 4th to 7th scale degrees, but most musicians find it difficult to associate the sound with scales because melodic skips of a tritone are not very numerous.
4. The tritone occurs in the diminished triad as well, but it too is not as common as either the major or minor triad.
5. Imagine the sound of a P5th and diminish that interval by a half-step.

6. Memorize the unique sound of the tritone. Listen to it many times until it is firmly entrenched in your mind. This way you will have instant access to it and will not have to think of it in relation to other intervals. It's not easy to do but the time spent will be well worth it.

The second note is above the first:

11.–30. (R)

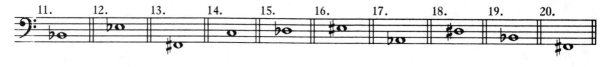

The second note is below the first:

31.–60. (R)

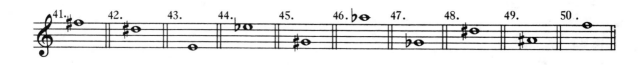

Harmony 5A

Chord Identification: I, ii, IV, and V Triads and Inversions

Each exercise consists of a series of four chords in block harmony.

In the blanks provided, write the analysis of each of the four chords.

Numbers 1–15 contain the following chords only (root-position):

FM: I   ii   IV   V

(R) 1. _____ _____ _____ _____   (R) 9. _____ _____ _____ _____

(R) 2. _____ _____ _____ _____   (R) 10. _____ _____ _____ _____

(R) 3. _____ _____ _____ _____   11. _____ _____ _____ _____

(R) 4. _____ _____ _____ _____   12. _____ _____ _____ _____

(R) 5. _____ _____ _____ _____   13. _____ _____ _____ _____

(R) 6. _____ _____ _____ _____   14. _____ _____ _____ _____

(R) 7. _____ _____ _____ _____   15. _____ _____ _____ _____

(R) 8. _____ _____ _____ _____

Numbers 16–25 contain the following chords only:

Dm: i   i^6 i$^6_4$ *ii^{o6} iv   iv^6 V   V^6

Numbers 16–25 contain inversions.

16. _____ _____ _____ _____   21. _____ _____ _____ _____

17. _____ _____ _____ _____   22. _____ _____ _____ _____

18. _____ _____ _____ _____   23. _____ _____ _____ _____

19. _____ _____ _____ _____   24. _____ _____ _____ _____

20. _____ _____ _____ _____   25. _____ _____ _____ _____

*The diminished supertonic triad is seldom found in root-position.

Harmony 5B

Harmonic Dictation: I, ii, IV, and V
Triads in Four-Part Chorale Phrases

Each exercise consists of a phrase from a chorale.

    Numbers 1–6:   All triads are in root position.

    Numbers 7–12:   Triads may be in inversions as well as root position.

1. Indicate the Roman numeral analysis of each triad in the blanks provided.
2. List any nonharmonic tones beneath the harmonic analysis.
3. If the instructor requests it, give the melodic line of both the soprano and bass voices.
4. If the instructor requests it, give the melodic line of both the alto and tenor voices.

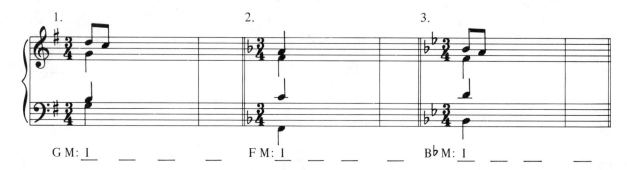

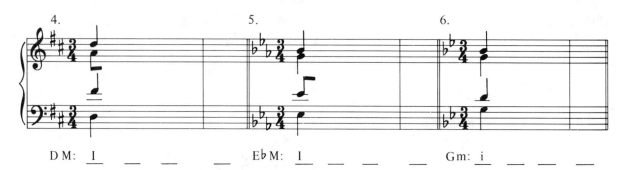

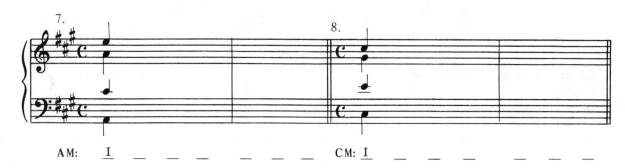

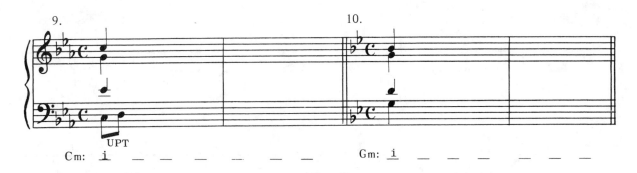

Cm: i _ _ _ _ _ _ _   Gm: i _ _ _ _ _ _ _

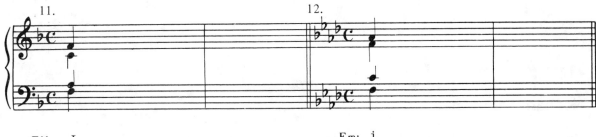

FM: I _ _ _ _ _ _ _   Fm: i _ _ _ _ _ _ _

Harmony 5C

Harmonic Rhythm and
Nonharmonic Tones

Each exercise consists of a phrase of **homophonic** music.

1. In each of the following five exercises you have been given the rhythm of the melody, numbers indicating the melody tones and circles around each number indicating a nonharmonic tone.
2. Place an "X" above each number where the harmony changes.
3. Above the circled numbers, indicate the *type* of each nonharmonic tone.

1.

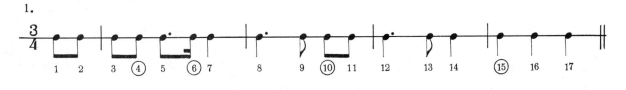

2.

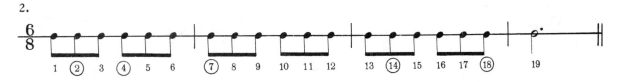

3.

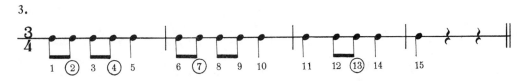

4.

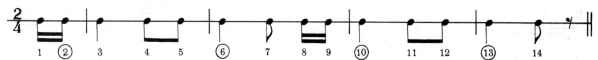

5.

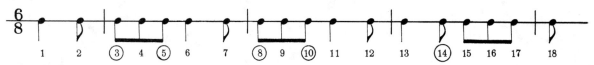

Harmony 5D

Nonharmonic Tones

Each exercise consists of two chords including a nonharmonic tone or tones.

1. Place the abbreviation indicating the nonharmonic tone in the blank provided.

   UPT = Unaccented passing tone   APP = Appoggiatura

   APT = Accented passing tone   ET = Escape tone

      S = Suspension   A = Anticipation

     NT = Neighboring tone

2. Exercises 1–10 consist of two chords including a nonharmonic tone.

   1. _____   6. _____

   2. _____   7. _____

   3. _____   8. _____

   4. _____   9. _____

   5. _____   10. _____

3. Exercises 11–20 contain two nonharmonic tones. List the nonharmonic tones in the upper voice first, in the lower voice second.

   11. _____   16. _____

   12. _____   17. _____

   13. _____   18. _____

   14. _____   19. _____

   15. _____   20. _____

Rhythm 5A

Rhythmic Dictation: Introduction
to Quarter-Beat Values

Each exercise is a short melodic phrase. Numbers 1–12 consist of two measures each and are intended to introduce quarter-beat values. Numbers 13–22 are taken from music literature.

Complete each rhythm on the single line provided. The value of the first note is given in all exercises.

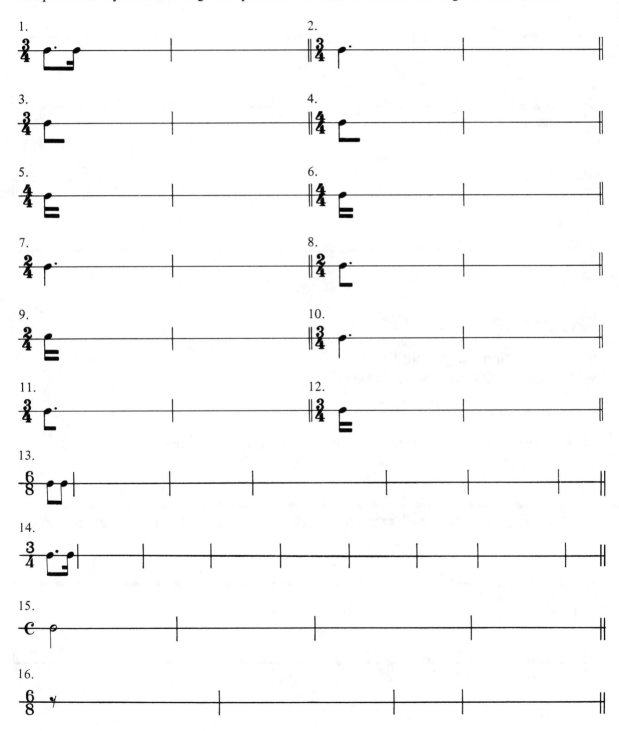

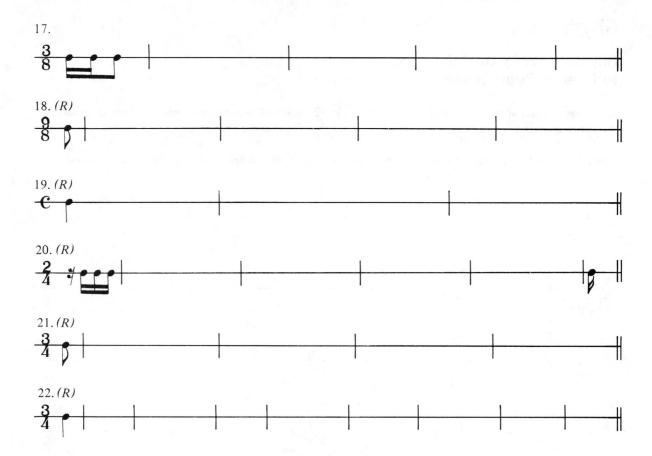

Rhythm 5B

Error Detection: Rhythmic Phrases
with Errors—Quarter-Beat Values

Each exercise contains a melodic phrase with one rhythmic error.

Circle the number representing the section of the phrase containing the rhythmic error.

4.

UNIT 6

Melody 6A

Melodic Dictation: Intervals of a 7th

Each exercise consists of a short melody. Numbers 1–10 introduce the intervals of a 7th, while numbers 11–18 are excerpted from the works of J. S. Bach.

1. After hearing each melody try immediately to sing it in its entirety in your mind (aural imagery).
2. When that is accomplished, add solfeggio syllables or numbers as you think the melody through again.
3. Do not write out the melody until you have completed these two important procedures.
4. Complete each melody on the staff in notation. The first note(s) are given for each.

In numbers 1–10 the given pitch is the tonic:

Melody 6B

Scales: Scale Degrees

1. The instructor first plays a scale, then three tones of that scale.
2. Identify the three scale degrees played.
3. The instructor will tell you whether to use scale numbers or syllables.

*(R) means recorded.

The instructor plays:

1. _____ _____ _____

2. _____ _____ _____

3. _____ _____ _____

4. _____ _____ _____

5. _____ _____ _____

6. _____ _____ _____

7. _____ _____ _____

8. _____ _____ _____

9. _____ _____ _____

10. _____ _____ _____

11. _____ _____ _____

12. _____ _____ _____

13. _____ _____ _____

14. _____ _____ _____

15. _____ _____ _____

16. _____ _____ _____

17. _____ _____ _____

18. _____ _____ _____

19. _____ _____ _____

20. _____ _____ _____

21. _____ _____ _____

22. _____ _____ _____

23. _____ _____ _____

24. _____ _____ _____

25. _____ _____ _____

26. _____ _____ _____

27. _____ _____ _____

28. _____ _____ _____

29. _____ _____ _____

30. _____ _____ _____

31. _____ _____ _____

32. _____ _____ _____

Melody 6C

Melodic Figure Identification:
Melodic Devices

Each exercise consists of a melodic phrase.

In the blank provided, write the type of device (below) found in each melody:

SEQUENCE   The immediate restating of a melodic figure at a higher or lower pitch
                            so that the structure of the figure is maintained. Each unit is called a
                            segment.

REPEATED MELODY   A segment of the melody is repeated with or without the same rhythm.

REPEATED RHYTHM   A rhythmic (but not melodic) figure is repeated.

Listen carefully to each melody as played and circle one of the four:

1. SEQUENCE   (when you hear a sequence)
2. REPEATED MELODY   (when you hear a melody repeated with or without the same rhythm)
3. REPEATED RHYTHM   (when you hear a rhythm (only) repeated—no repeated melody or sequence)
4. NONE   (when you hear none of the three devices listed above)

1. SEQUENCE	REPEATED MELODY	REPEATED RHYTHM	NONE
2. SEQUENCE	REPEATED MELODY	REPEATED RHYTHM	NONE
3. SEQUENCE	REPEATED MELODY	REPEATED RHYTHM	NONE
(R)4. SEQUENCE	REPEATED MELODY	REPEATED RHYTHM	NONE
(R)5. SEQUENCE	REPEATED MELODY	REPEATED RHYTHM	NONE
(R)6. SEQUENCE	REPEATED MELODY	REPEATED RHYTHM	NONE
(R)7. SEQUENCE	REPEATED MELODY	REPEATED RHYTHM	NONE
(R)8. SEQUENCE	REPEATED MELODY	REPEATED RHYTHM	NONE

Melody 6D

New Intervals: m7 and M7

Intervals studied to date: m2, M2, m3, M3, P4, P5, m6, M6, A4, D5

Each exercise consists of a single interval. The first note is given.

1. Write the second note of the interval on the staff.
2. Place the name of the interval in the blank provided.
3. The best way to identify both the major and minor 7th is to practice singing them above and below a variety of given pitches. Soon you will have them well in mind and can recognize their peculiar qualities without having to rely on a special system.
4. Another method, of short term benefit, is to think of major and minor 7ths as inversions of minor or major seconds—easier to identify. Sing an octave above or below (depending on the situation) to get into proper range. Then, sing up or down a half- or whole-step to complete the original major or minor 7th.

The missing note is above the given note:

11.–30. (R)

The missing note is below the given note:

Harmony 6A

Chord Identification: I, ii, IV, V, and vi Triads

Each exercise consists of four block chords in four-part harmony.

Write the Roman numeral analysis of each chord in the blanks provided.

Numbers 1–15 contain root-position triads only:

(R) 1. _____ _____ _____ _____   *(R)* 4. _____ _____ _____ _____

(R) 2. _____ _____ _____ _____   *(R)* 5. _____ _____ _____ _____

(R) 3. _____ _____ _____ _____   *(R)* 6. _____ _____ _____ _____

(R) 7. ___ ___ ___ ___   12. ___ ___ ___ ___

(R) 8. ___ ___ ___ ___   13. ___ ___ ___ ___

(R) 9. ___ ___ ___ ___   14. ___ ___ ___ ___

(R)10. ___ ___ ___ ___   15. ___ ___ ___ ___

11. ___ ___ ___ ___

Numbers 16–25 contain inversions:

16. ___ ___ ___ ___   21. ___ ___ ___ ___

17. ___ ___ ___ ___   22. ___ ___ ___ ___

18. ___ ___ ___ ___   23. ___ ___ ___ ___

19. ___ ___ ___ ___   24. ___ ___ ___ ___

20. ___ ___ ___ ___   25. ___ ___ ___ ___

Harmony 6B

Harmonic Dictation: I, ii, IV (iv), V, and vi (or VI) Triads in Four-Part Chorale Phrases

Each exercise consists of a chorale phrase. Numbers 7–14 are harmonizations by Bach.

Numbers 1–6:   All triads are in root position.

Numbers 7–14:   Triads may be in inversions as well as root position.

1. Indicate the Roman numeral analysis of each triad in the blanks provided.
2. List any nonharmonic tones beneath the harmonic analysis.
3. If the instructor requests it, give the melodic line of both the soprano and bass voices.
4. If the instructor requests it, give the melodic line of both the alto and tenor voices.

F M: I ___ ___ ___   D M: I ___ ___ ___   G m: i ___ ___ ___

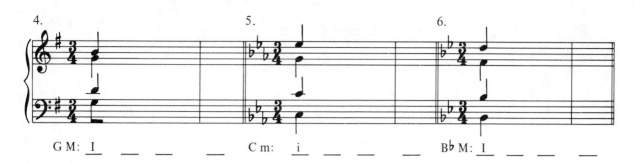

GM: I _ _ _ _ _   Cm: i _ _ _ _   B♭M: I _ _ _ _ _

FM: I _ _ _ _ _   GM: I _

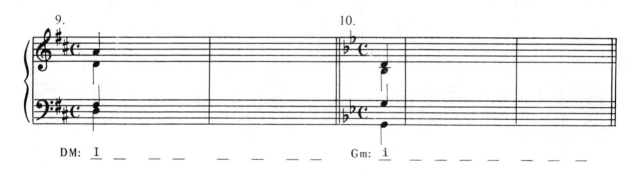

DM: I _ _ _ _ _   Gm: i _ _

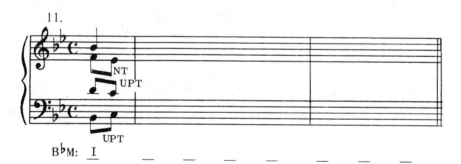

B♭M: I _ _ _ _ _

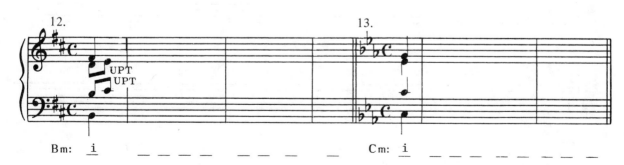

Bm: i _ _ _ _ _   Cm: i _

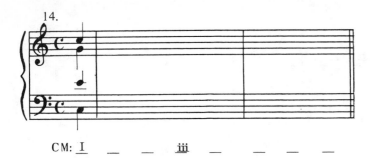

CM: I _ _ iii _ _ _ _

Harmony 6C

Harmonic Dictation: Harmonic Rhythm
and Analysis—I, ii, IV, V, vi

Each exercise consists of a phrase of music in homophonic single-melody with chordal accompaniment style.

1. Write the harmonic rhythm by bracketing the numbers.
2. Write the harmonic analysis above each bracket.
3. Write the melody on the staff in notation if the instructor requests you to do so.

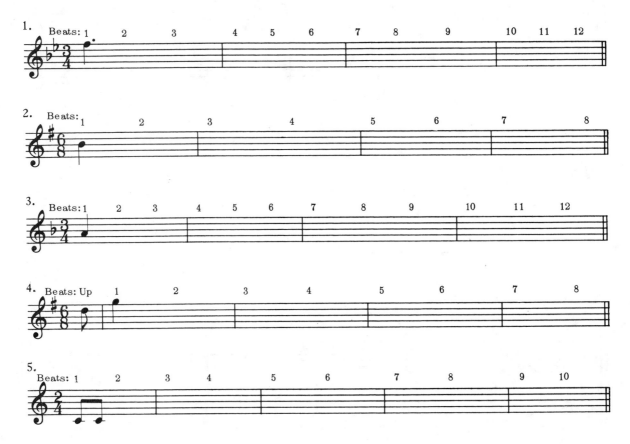

Harmony 6D

Chord Identification: Major, Minor, Diminished, and Augmented Triads

Each exercise consists of a single triad in four-part harmony.

1. The notes written are on the correct line or space, but may require accidentals to make them conform to what is played.
2. If the triad as written is not the same as the one you hear, add the necessary accidentals to make it conform.
3. The bass note is *always* correct.

The examples illustrate the correct procedure:

EXAMPLES:

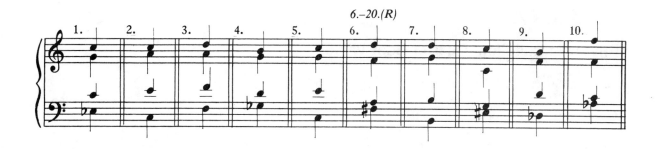

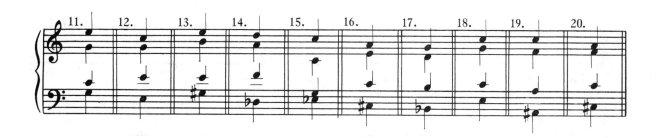

Harmony 6E

Error Detection: Triads in Four Parts

Each exercise consists of two triads in four parts.

As played by the instructor, one note in each exercise is incorrect. Any voice may contain an error.

1. Indicate the chord (no. 1 or no. 2) containing the error.
2. Indicate the voice containing the error:
   S = Soprano   A = Alto   T = Tenor   B = Bass

The example indicates the correct procedure.

Rhythm 6A

Rhythmic Dictation: Quarter-Beat Values

Each exercise consists of a two-measure melody.

Complete the rhythm on a neutral pitch.

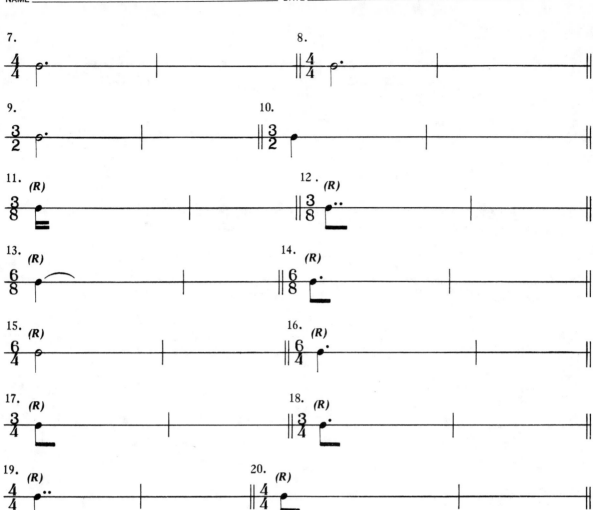

Rhythm 6B

Error Detection: Triplet Figures

Each exercise consists of a melodic phrase. Most phrases contain triplet figures.

In one of the measures, the written rhythm will not agree with the version played.

Circle the number representing the measure with the "error."

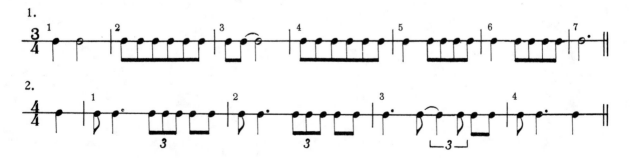

UNIT 7

Melody 7A

Error Detection

Each exercise consists of a phrase of music by Schubert.

Circle the numbers representing the three pitches that are different from those played.

Melody 7B

Melodic Dictation: Two-Phrase Melodies

Each exercise is a melody composed of two phrases. The second phrase begins immediately after the | |, marked in each melody.

1. Complete each melody on the staff in notation. The first note(s) of each phrase is given.
2. As you hear the melody, try to memorize each phrase so that you can sing it accurately in your mind.
3. Think of the scale degree each pitch represents by including solfeggio syllables or numbers.
4. When all pitches are accounted for, you are ready to write the phrase on the staff.

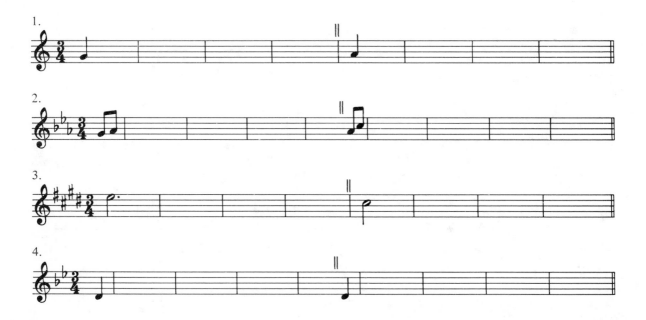

Melody 7C

Harmonic Rhythm, Harmonic Analysis, Sequences, Phrase Relationships, and Cadences

Each exercise consists of two phrases excerpted from a Chopin mazurka.

HARMONIC RHYTHM   Place an "X" above each number where a chord change occurs. The chords found in each exercise are listed. To prepare for the exercise, play and sing each chord until it is familiar.

HARMONIC ANALYSIS   Place the Roman numeral analysis of each chord below the appropriate numbers. As you listen, keep looking at the list of possible chords and sketch the numbers where each chord occurs. Then, after a few listenings, you are ready to transfer the analysis to the requested position.

CADENCES   Indicate the cadence types in the blanks provided. By this time you will have placed all chord analyses above the numbers and can assess the cadence type.

*(R) means recorded.

	Phrase 1	Phrase 2

MELODIC SEQUENCES Bracket the numbers where a melodic sequence is heard. This is a separate operation. All of these Chopin examples are homophonic (a single melodic line, easily distinguished) and the melody is in the highest sounding voice. Listen for a melodic excerpt that is sounded more than once but at different scale locations.

PHRASE RELATIONSHIP Indicate the type of phrase relationship (repeated, modified repeated, parallel, or contrasting) in the blank provided.

		Phrase 1	Phrase 2	
Repeated—	If 2nd phrase repeats the 1st—	A	A	
Modified repeated—	If 2nd phrase repeats the 1st but is slightly modified—	A	A′	
Parallel—	If 2nd phrase is parallel to 1st—	A	A′	(or AP)
Contrasting—	If 2nd phrase is contrasting to 1st—	A	B	
Melodic Dictation (optional)	Write the melody (highest voice on the blank staff).			

1. Key: C Major chords: I I$_4^6$ IV^6 V

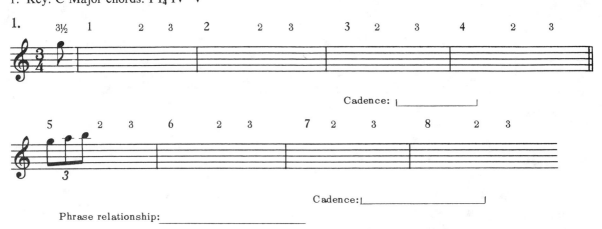

Phrase relationship: _____

2. Key: B Major chords: ii^6 V I

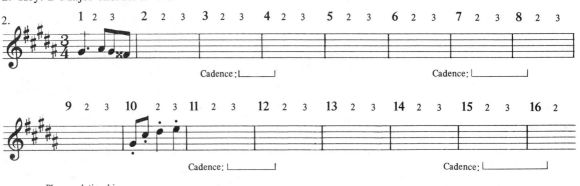

Phrase relationship: _____

3. Key: Bb Major chords: I IV V VI

Cadence: |_____| Cadence: |_____|

Phrase relationship: _____

4. Key: Bb Major chords: I IV V

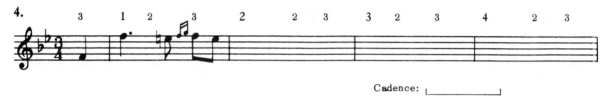

Cadence: |_____|

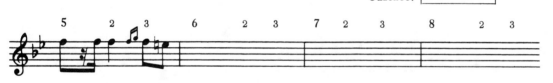

Cadence: |_____|

Phrase relationship: _____

5. Key: F Major chords: I IV$^6_4$ V

Cadence: | No Cadence |

Cadence: |_____|

Phrase relationship: _____

6. Key: D Major chords: I ii⁶ V

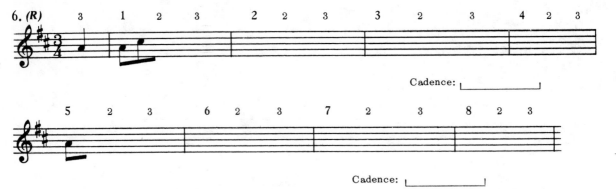

Cadence: ⌐_____⌐

Cadence: ⌐_____⌐

Phrase relationship: _____

7. Key: C Major chords: I ii V

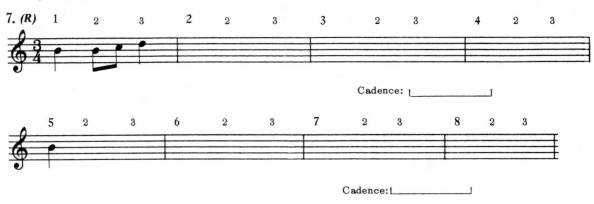

Cadence: ⌐_____⌐

Cadence: ⌐_____⌐

Phrase relationship: _____

8. Key: A♭ Major chords: I I⁶₄ IV V

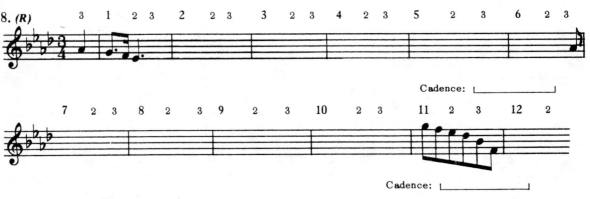

Cadence: ⌐_____⌐

Cadence: ⌐_____⌐

Phrase relationship: _____

Melody 7D

Intervals: Major and Natural Minor Scales

Each exercise consists of a single interval (two tones).

1. Write the name of the interval in the blank provided.
2. Write the second note of the interval on the staff in notation.
3. If you have difficulty identifying particular intervals review them thoroughly before undertaking this section. For locating helpful strategy:

Unit	Type	Section	Page	Strategy for Particular Intervals					
1	Melody	D	4	m2	M2	m3	M3		
2	Melody	D	14	P5	P4				
3	Melody	E	27	m2	M2	m3	M3	P5	P4
4	Melody	D	41	m6	M6				
5	Melody	D	55	Tritone					
6	Melody	D	68	m7	M7				

The given tone is the lower note of the interval.

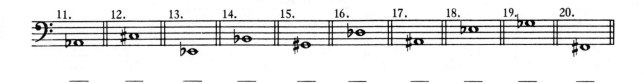

The given note is the upper note of the interval:

31.–60. (R)

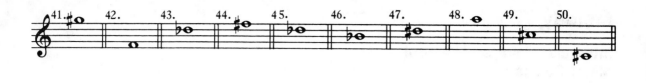

Harmony 7A

Chord Identification: I, ii, iii, IV, V, and vi Triads and Inversions

Each exercise consists of a series of four chords in block harmony.

In the blanks provided write the analysis of each of the four chords.

Numbers 1–10 contain the following chords only:

A major: I   ii   iii   IV   V   vi

Numbers 1–10 contain root-position triads only:

(R) 1. _____ _____ _____ _____   (R) 6. _____ _____ _____ _____

(R) 2. _____ _____ _____ _____   (R) 7. _____ _____ _____ _____

(R) 3. _____ _____ _____ _____   (R) 8. _____ _____ _____ _____

(R) 4. _____ _____ _____ _____   (R) 9. _____ _____ _____ _____

(R) 5. _____ _____ _____ _____   (R)10. _____ _____ _____ _____

For numbers 11–20 contain the following chords only:

A minor: i   i⁶   ii⁶   III   III⁶   III+   III+⁶   iv   iv⁶   V   V⁶   VI   VI⁶

Numbers 11–20 contain inversions:

11. _____ _____ _____ _____   16. _____ _____ _____ _____

12. _____ _____ _____ _____   17. _____ _____ _____ _____

13. _____ _____ _____ _____   18. _____ _____ _____ _____

14. _____ _____ _____ _____   19. _____ _____ _____ _____

15. _____ _____ _____ _____   20. _____ _____ _____ _____

Harmony 7B

Nonharmonic Tones

Each exercise consists of a short excerpt in four-part harmony from a Bach chorale.

Each exercise contains two, three, or four nonharmonic tones. The rhythm (only) is given.

Circle the nonharmonic tones, and write the abbreviations representing the types in the blanks provided. Keep the order the same as in the excerpt. Each exercise is numbered for greater ease in class discussions.

Abbreviations:

UPT	= UNACCENTED PASSING TONE	APP	= APPOGGIATURA
APT	= ACCENTED PASSING TONE	SUS	= SUSPENSION
NT	= NEIGHBORING TONE	A	= ANTICIPATION
ET	= ESCAPE TONE		

EXAMPLE:

The instructor plays:

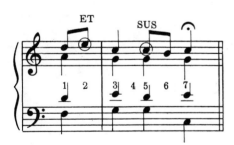

The *rhythm* given for you is:

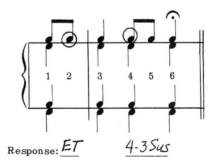

Response: *ET   4-3 Sus*

Harmony 7C

Harmonic Dictation: I, ii, IV (iv), V, and vi (or VI) Triads in Four-Part Chorale Phrases

Each exercise consists of a chorale phrase.

Numbers	Harmony Included	Positions
1–6	All listed above	Root position exclusively
7–12	All listed above except vi (VI). An occasional vii	Root position and inversions

1. Indicate the Roman numeral analysis of each Triad in the blanks provided.
2. List nonharmonic tones beneath the harmonic analysis.
3. If the instructor requests it, give the melodic line of both the soprano and bass voices.
4. If the instructor requests it, give the melodic line of both the alto and tenor voices.

Harmony 7D

Error Detection: Errors in Four-Part Writing

Each exercise consists of two chords. In the second chord, one of the four tones is not played as written.

Indicate the error in the second chord by circling the note.

10.–18. (R)

Rhythm 7A

Rhythmic Dictation: Rhythmic Figures Including Quarter-Beat Values

Each exercise consists of two measures of 2/4, 3/4, 4/4, or 6/8 meter.

1. For numbers 1–10 the meter signature and first note value is given.
2. For numbers 11–20 nothing is given, but the instructor will provide the basic beat before beginning.

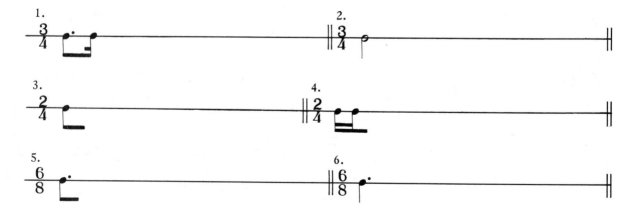

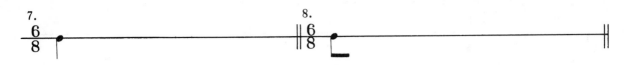

7.
$\frac{6}{8}$

8.
$\frac{6}{8}$

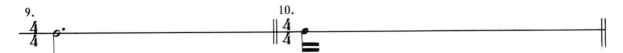

9.
$\frac{4}{4}$

10.
$\frac{4}{4}$

3. Listen for the instructor to provide the basic beat. Then, indicate:
   1. The meter signature
   2. The rhythm on the staff using a neutral pitch

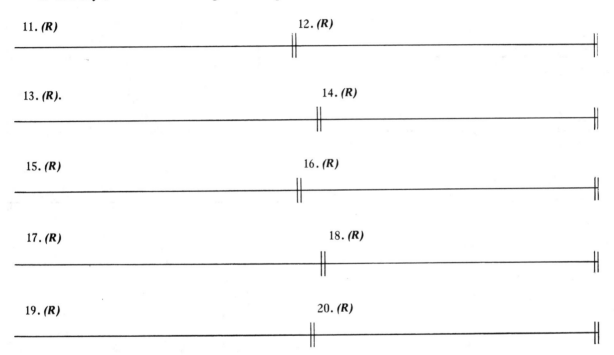

11. *(R)*   12. *(R)*

13. *(R)*.   14. *(R)*

15. *(R)*   16. *(R)*

17. *(R)*   18. *(R)*

19. *(R)*   20. *(R)*

Rhythm 7B

Rhythmic Dictation: Beat Units
Divided into Triplets

Each exercise consists of a short phrase of music.

Indicate the rhythm on the staff using a neutral pitch.

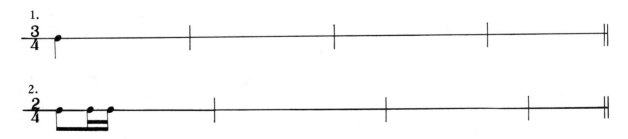

1.
$\frac{3}{4}$

2.
$\frac{2}{4}$

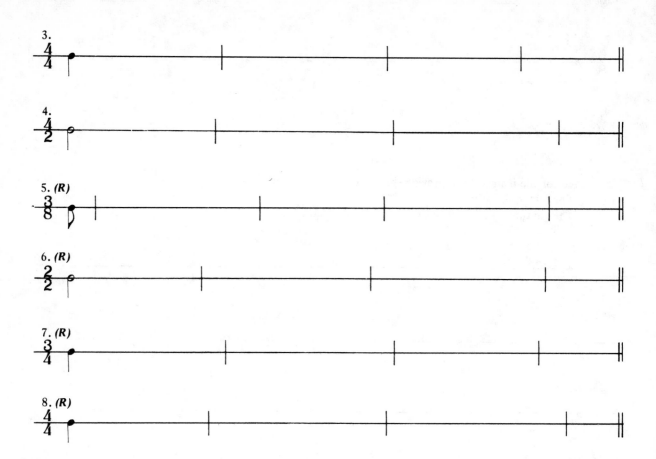

UNIT 8

Melody 8A

Melodic Dictation: Larger Leaps

Each exercise consists of a short two-measure melody.

Complete each melody on the staff in notation.

*(R) means recorded.

Melody 8B

Error Detection

Each exercise consists of a phrase of music by Handel and contains three pitch errors.

Place a circle around the numbers that represent pitches different from those played.

7. *(R)*

1 2 3 4 5 6 7 8 9 10 11 12 13 14 15 16 17 18 19 20 21 22

8. *(R)*

1 2 3 4 5 6 7 8 9 10 11 12 13 14 15 16 17 18 19

9. *(R)*

1 2 3 4 5 6 7 8 9 10 11 12 13 14 15 16 17 18 19 20 21 22 23 24 25 26 27 28 29 30 31 32 33

10. *(R)*

1 2 3 4 5 6 7 8 9 10 11 12 13 14 15 16 17 18 19 20 21 22 23

Melody 8C

Melodic Dictation: Two-Part Dictation

Each exercise consists of a short two-voiced melodic composition.

Complete the missing tones on the staff in notation.

1.

2.

3.

4.

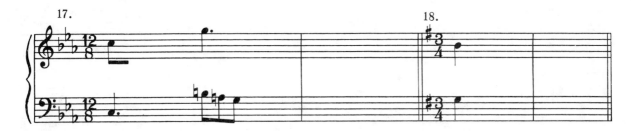

Melody 8D

Intervals

Each exercise consists of a single melodic interval.

1. Write the name of the interval in the blank provided.
2. Write the remaining note of the interval on the staff.

The given note is the lower of the two:

The given note is the upper of the two:

31.–60. (R)

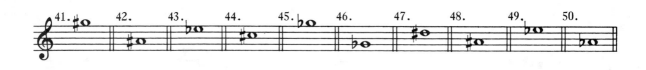

Harmony 8A

Chord Identification: Diatonic Triads

Each exercise consists of four chords in block harmony.

Write the Roman numeral analysis of each chord in the blank provided.

Numbers 1–15 use I, ii, iii, IV, V, vi

Numbers 1–15 contain root-position triads only:

(R) 1. _____ _____ _____ _____	*(R)* 7. _____ _____ _____ _____
(R) 2. _____ _____ _____ _____	*(R)* 8. _____ _____ _____ _____
(R) 3. _____ _____ _____ _____	*(R)* 9. _____ _____ _____ _____
(R) 4. _____ _____ _____ _____	*(R)*10. _____ _____ _____ _____
(R) 5. _____ _____ _____ _____	11. _____ _____ _____ _____
(R) 6. _____ _____ _____ _____	12. _____ _____ _____ _____

13. _____ _____ _____ _____   15. _____ _____ _____ _____

14. _____ _____ _____ _____

Numbers 16–25 contain   I, ii, iii, IV, V, vi
                               I⁶, ii⁶, iii⁶, IV⁶, V⁶, vi⁶, vii°⁶

F M: I   I 6   ii   ii 6   iii   iii 6   IV   IV 6   V   V 6   vi   vi 6   vii o 6

Numbers 16–25 contain inversions:

16. _____ _____ _____ _____   21. _____ _____ _____ _____

17. _____ _____ _____ _____   22. _____ _____ _____ _____

18. _____ _____ _____ _____   23. _____ _____ _____ _____

19. _____ _____ _____ _____   24. _____ _____ _____ _____

20. _____ _____ _____ _____   25. _____ _____ _____ _____

Harmony 8B

Harmonic Dictation: Diatonic Triads
in Four-Part Chorale Phrases

Each exercise consists of a chorale phrase.

1. Phrases 1–6—contain only four root position triads each. Nonharmonic tones are limited to unaccented passing tones and an occasional suspension.
2. Phrases 7–14—contain seven triads each in any position. Nonharmonic tones are: UPT, APT, ET, and 4–3 suspensions.
3. Indicate the Roman numeral analysis of each triad in the blanks provided.
4. List nonharmonic tones beneath the harmonic analysis.
5. If the instructor requests it, give the melodic line of both the soprano and bass voices.
6. If the instructor requests it, give the melodic line of both the alto and tenor voices.

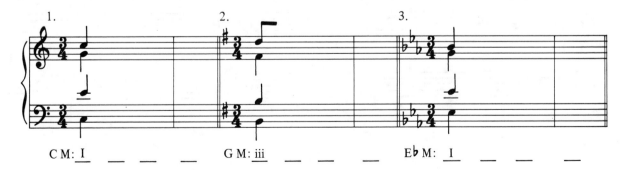

C M: I   ___ ___ ___   G M: iii   ___ ___ ___   E♭ M: I   ___ ___ ___

Harmony 8C

Harmonic Dictation: Harmonic Rhythm and Analysis of Familiar Melodies

Each exercise consists of a phrase in four-part harmony from a familiar melody.

1. Indicate the melody on the staff in notation.
2. Bracket the melody tones within each basic harmony to show the harmonic rhythm.
3. Indicate the harmonic analysis of each bracketed area above the bracket. (If more than one position of a chord occurs within a bracket, indicate the one with the *lowest* sounding tone.)
4. Circle and name any nonharmonic tones. Use abbreviations.

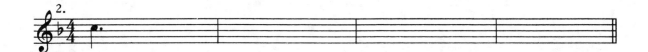

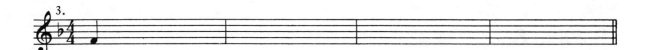

Harmony 8D

Error Detection: Errors in Triads

Each exercise consists of two triads in four parts.

As played by the instructor, *one* note in each exercise is incorrect. Any voice may contain an error.

1. Indicate the chord (no. 1 or no. 2) containing the error.
2. Indicate also the voice where the error occurs:
   S = Soprano   A = Alto   T = Tenor   B = Bass

The example indicates the correct procedure.

Ex.
Chord: 2   ____ ____ ____ ____ ____ ____ ____ ____ ____

Voice: A   ____ ____ ____ ____ ____ ____ ____ ____ ____

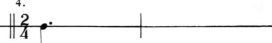

Rhythm 8A

Rhythmic Dictation: Quarter-Beat Values

Each exercise consists of a two-measure melody.

Complete each rhythm on a neutral pitch.

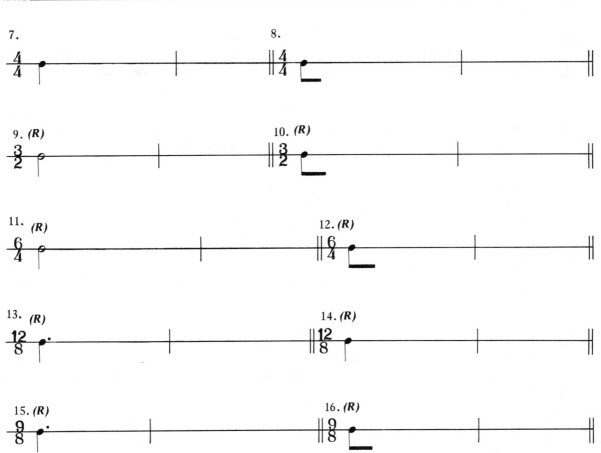

Rhythm 8B

Error Detection: Quarter-Beat Values

Each exercise consists of a melodic phrase from music literature in which one rhythmic error exists.

Circle the number that indicates the area of the error.

UNIT 9

Melody 9A

Melodic Dictation: Short Melodies
from Music Literature

Each exercise consists of a short melodic excerpt from music literature.

Complete each melody on the staff in notation.

*(R) means recorded.

Melody 9B

Error Detection

Each exercise consists of a phrase of music by César Franck.

Place a circle around the three numbers that represent pitches different from those played.

1.

2.

3.

4.

5.

6.

7.

8.

9.

10.

Melody 9C

Error Detection: Two-Voiced Compositions

Each exercise consists of a short excerpt from compositions by the Baroque composers J. S. Bach and G. P. Telemann.

1. Each excerpt contains *three* pitch errors.
2. The notes of each composition are numbered.
3. Circle the numbers representing incorrect pitches (as played).
4. The first note of each voice in all exercises is correct.

Melody 9D

Harmonic Intervals

1. Immediately after hearing the interval, sing both pitches: lower to upper for numbers 1–30 and upper to lower for numbers 31–60.
2. Harmonic intervals (both pitches sound together) are considered more difficult than melodic (one note then the other) because the two tend to fuse into a single homogenized effect.
3. Separating the two into distinct pitches helps considerably in recognizing and identifying the interval, but remember that this procedure is temporary.
4. Gradually you must learn to identify intervals directly without going through the intermediary step. Use the crutch for a while, and at the same time keep trying to graduate to the next level.
5. Write the remaining note of the interval on the staff.
6. Write the name of the interval in the blank provided.

The given note is the lower of the two:

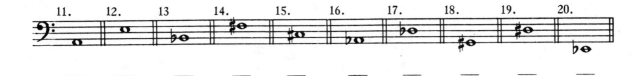

The given note is the upper of the two:

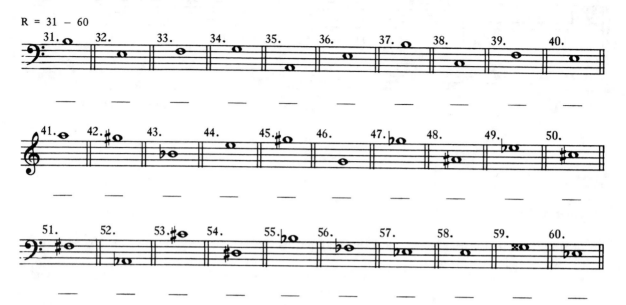

R = 31 – 60

Harmony 9A:

Chord Identification: $^6_4$ Chord

Each exercise consists of a series of four chords in block harmony.

Indicate:

1. The analysis of each of the four chords in the blanks provided
2. The type of $^6_4$ chord:

CADENTIAL   The tonic $^6_4$ chord resolves to the V chord at the cadence.

ii⁶ I$^6_4$ V I

PASSING BASS

The lowest tone (usually bass) acts as a passing tone between two triads, often between a triad and its inversion.

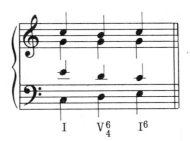

$$I \quad V_4^6 \quad I^6$$

NEIGHBORING TONE, or STATIONARY BASS

The bass tone is preceded and followed by the same tone and is interposed between two root-positions of the same triad.

$$V \quad I_4^6 \quad V$$

ARPEGGIATED BASS

The bass participates in an arpeggiation of a chord.

$$I \quad I^6 \quad I_4^6 \quad I$$

The following illustration indicates the correct procedure:

EXAMPLE:

Instructor plays:

$$I \quad IV \quad I_4^6 \quad V$$

Response:

	I	IV	I_4^6	V
	_____	_____	_____	_____

_____ Cadential _____
TYPE

1. _____ _____ _____ _____   10. _____ _____ _____ _____

_____   _____
TYPE   TYPE

2. _____ _____ _____ _____   (R)11. _____ _____ _____ _____

_____   _____
TYPE   TYPE

3. _____ _____ _____ _____   (R)12. _____ _____ _____ _____

_____   _____
TYPE   TYPE

4. _____ _____ _____ _____   (R)13. _____ _____ _____ _____

_____   _____
TYPE   TYPE

5. _____ _____ _____ _____   (R)14. _____ _____ _____ _____

_____   _____
TYPE   TYPE

6. _____ _____ _____ _____   (R)15. _____ _____ _____ _____

_____   _____
TYPE   TYPE

7. _____ _____ _____ _____   (R)16. _____ _____ _____ _____

_____   _____
TYPE   TYPE

8. _____ _____ _____ _____   (R)17. _____ _____ _____ _____

_____   _____
TYPE   TYPE

9. _____ _____ _____ _____   (R)18. _____ _____ _____ _____

_____   _____
TYPE   TYPE

*(R)*19. _____ _____ _____ _____   *(R)*20. _____ _____ _____ _____

_____   _____
                    TYPE   TYPE

Harmony 9B

Aspects of Two-Phrase Excerpts

PARALLEL PHRASES   Two phrases having an exactly similar beginning and standing in question-and-answer, or antecedent-and-consequent relationship, to form a complete period (first phrase ending on a half cadence, second phrase ending with an authentic cadence). Modified parallel phrases have somewhat less exact similarity in their beginnings.

CONTRASTING PHRASES   Two phrases also exhibiting a question-and-answer relationship, but dissimilar in their beginnings.

ALBERTI BASS   Stereotyped broken-chord accompaniment figures in the left-hand parts of eighteenth-century keyboard music.

Each following exercise consists of two phrases from a Haydn piano sonata containing parallel phrases, contrasting phrases, or Alberti bass.

1. Listen carefully three or four times to each excerpt and then circle the letter of all true statements.

The instructor now plays no. 1.

    a. The first phrase begins with tonic harmony while the second begins with dominant harmony.
    b. The two phrases are of contrasting type.
    c. A five-tone rhythmic motive is heard twice in each phrase.
    d. The two phrases are in modified parallel construction.
    e. Both phrases contain imitation.
    f. Both phrases contain only tonic and dominant harmony.
    g. Both phrases are homophonic.
    h. The first phrase has a prominent 7–6 suspension.
    i. The second phrase has a prominent 4–3 suspension.
    j. The last phrase ends with tonic harmony.
    k. Both phrases have the same cadence types.
    l. Both phrases have the same rhythm.
    m. The second phrase is a repetition of the first with the mode changed.
    n. The second phrase contains a sequence.
    o. The second phrase contains an extension.

The instructor now plays no. 2.

2. Circle the letter of all true statements.
    a. The basic harmony is tonic and dominant only.
    b. The basic harmony is tonic, supertonic, and dominant only.
    c. The basic harmony is subdominant and dominant only.
    d. The basic harmony is tonic and subdominant only.
    e. The basic harmony is tonic, supertonic, subdominant, and dominant only.
    f. The texture is polyphonic.

g. The excerpt contains a change of mode.
h. The excerpt contains an Alberti bass figure.
i. The second phrase contains an extension.
j. The most prominent nonharmonic device is the suspension.

3. Circle the letter (a–e) that indicates the correct harmonic rhythm. Each "X" indicates the beginning of a different harmony (the rhythm of the melody is reproduced for convenience).

The instructor now plays no. 3. (R)

4. Circle the letter of all true statements. The basic harmony in this excerpt is:
   a. Tonic and subdominant only.
   b. Tonic, subdominant, and dominant only.
   c. Tonic, supertonic, and dominant only.
   d. Tonic and dominant only.
   e. Tonic, supertonic, subdominant, and dominant only.

5. Circle the true statements regarding the excerpt (assuming two phrases):
   a. The most prominent nonharmonic tone is the suspension.
   b. The texture is polyphonic.
   c. The second phrase contains an extension.
   d. The first phrase is a sequence made up of two legs.
   e. The excerpt contains a change of mode.
   f. The harmonic rhythm is fast, consisting of at least ten changes per phrase.
   g. The phrases are in modified repeated relationship.
   h. The first phrase emphasizes tonic harmony while the second contrasts both subdominant and dominant harmony.
   i. The same type of cadence punctuates both phrases.
   j. A prominent false sequence appears in both phrases.

The instructor now plays no. 4.(R)

6. Circle the letter of all true statements. The basic chords in this excerpt are:
   a. Tonic, subdominant, and dominant only.
   b. Tonic and subdominant only.
   c. Tonic, supertonic, and dominant only.
   d. Tonic and dominant only.
   e. Tonic, submediant, and dominant only.

7. Assuming two phrases, the two cadences are (in order of appearance):
   a. Half and authentic.
   b. Authentic and authentic.
   c. Authentic and half.
   d. Half and half.
   e. Plagal and authentic.

8. Assuming two phrases, the relationship between the two could be construed logically in two ways:
   a. Either modified repeated or parallel.
   b. Either contrasting or parallel.
   c. Either exact repeated or parallel.
   d. Either exact or modified repeated.
   e. Either contrasting or modified repeated.

Harmony 9C

Nonharmonic Tones

Each exercise consists of a short excerpt from a four-voiced chorale by Bach.

1. On neutral pitches, the rhythm of each exercise is given.
2. Nonharmonic tones are marked "X" and numbered.
3. Listen carefully to each excerpt; then, write the type of each nonharmonic tone in the blank provided.

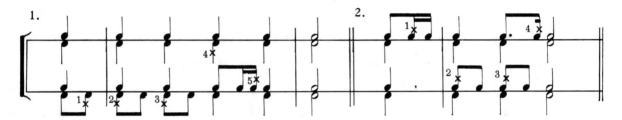

Exercise 1.

1. _____

2. _____

3. _____

4. _____

5. _____

Exercise 2.

1. _____

2. _____

3. _____

4. _____

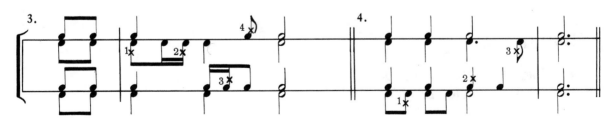

Exercise 3.

1. _____

2. _____

3. _____

4. _____

Exercise 4.

1. _____

2. _____

3. _____

Exercise 5.

1. _____

2. _____

3. _____

Exercise 6.

1. _____

2. _____

3. _____

4. _____

5. _____

Exercise 7.

1. _____

2. _____

3. _____

4. _____

Exercise 8.

1. _____

2. _____

3. _____

Rhythm 9A

Rhythmic Dictation: Compound
Meters with Quarter-Beat Values

Each exercise is a short, two-measure melodic excerpt. The meter signature and beginning durational value is given.

Complete each rhythm on a neutral pitch.

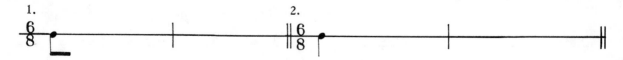

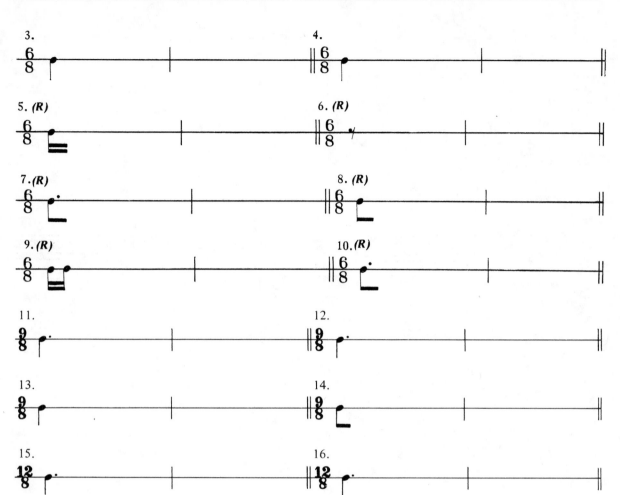

UNIT 10

Melody 10A

Phrase Relationships and Cadences

Each exercise consists of a number of phrases of homophonic music.

1. Identify the number of phrases in each excerpt.
2. Identify the relationship of the phrases to each other (using letters). Use "P" after a letter to indicate a parallel relationship.
3. Identify the types of cadences at the end of each phrase.
4. Optional: Write the first phrase on the staff in notation.

1.

Number of phrases   Phrase relationships   Type of cadence at the end of each phrase (in order of appearance)

2.

Number of phrases   Phrase relationships   Type of cadence at the end of each phrase (in order of appearance)

3.

Number of phrases   Phrase relationships   Type of cadence at the end of each phrase (in order of appearance)

4.

Number of phrases   Phrase relationships   Type of cadence at the end of each phrase (in order of appearance)

(R)*5.

Number of phrases   Phrase relationships   Type of cadence at the end of each phrase (in order of appearance)

(R) 6.

Number of phrases   Phrase relationships   Type of cadence at the end of each phrase (in order of appearance)

(R) 7.

Number of phrases   Phrase relationships   Type of cadence at the end of each phrase (in order of appearance)

*(R) means recorded.

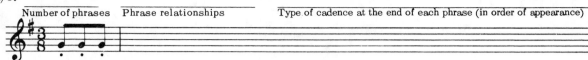

Number of phrases	Phrase relationships		Type of cadence at the end of each phrase (in order of appearance)

Melody 10B

Error Detection

Each exercise consists of a phrase of music by Bach.

Place a circle around the three numbers that represent pitches different from those played.

8.

9.

10.

Melody 10C

Melodic Dictation: Sequences

Each exercise consists of eight tones, four of which are given.

Write the remaining four tones on the staff in notation.

Diatonic sequences with no accidentals:

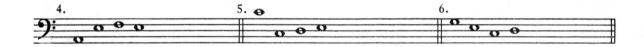

Diatonic sequences:

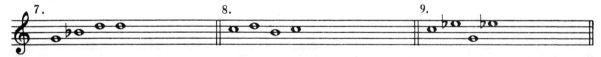

11.—21.(R)

Nondiatonic sequences:

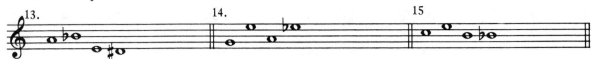

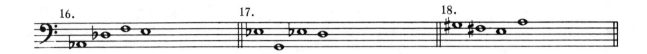

Melody 10D

Intervals: Harmonic Intervals of the m3, Tritone, P5, m6, M6, and m7

Each exercise consists of a single interval. The first note of the interval is the lower note of the two.

1. Indicate the name of the interval in the blank provided.
2. Indicate the remaining note of the interval on the staff.

The given note is the lower of the two.

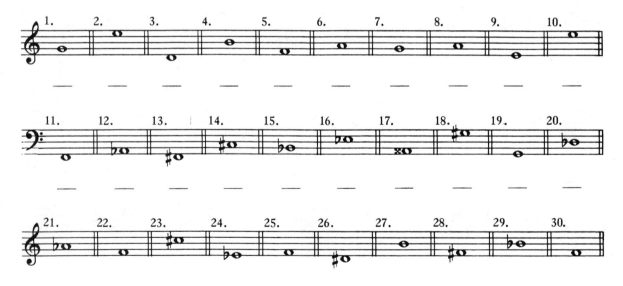

The give note is the upper of the two.

31.–60.(R)

Harmony 10A

Chord Identification: Dominant
7th Chord and Inversions

Each exercise consists of a series of four chords in block harmony.

1. Analyze each of the four chords in the blanks provided.
2. The V⁷ is the only new chord introduced in this unit. It is analyzed as follows:

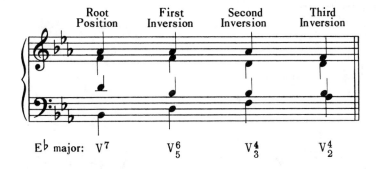

3. Write the analysis in the blanks provided.

Numbers 1–15 contain root-position chords only:

(R) 1. _____ _____ _____ _____   *(R)* 5. _____ _____ _____ _____

(R) 2. _____ _____ _____ _____   *(R)* 6. _____ _____ _____ _____

(R) 3. _____ _____ _____ _____   *(R)* 7. _____ _____ _____ _____

(R) 4. _____ _____ _____ _____   *(R)* 8. _____ _____ _____ _____

(R) 9. (R) 9. ___ ___ ___ ___   13. ___ ___ ___ ___

(R)10. ___ ___ ___ ___   14. ___ ___ ___ ___

11. ___ ___ ___ ___   15. ___ ___ ___ ___

12. ___ ___ ___ ___

Numbers 16–25 contain inversions:

16. ___ ___ ___ ___   21. ___ ___ ___ ___

17. ___ ___ ___ ___   22. ___ ___ ___ ___

18. ___ ___ ___ ___   23. ___ ___ ___ ___

19. ___ ___ ___ ___   24. ___ ___ ___ ___

20. ___ ___ ___ ___   25. ___ ___ ___ ___

Harmony 10B

Error Detection: Triads or Dominant 7th Chords

Each exercise consists of two chords.

As played by the instructor, one note in each exercise is incorrect. Any voice may contain an error.

1. Indicate the chord (no. 1 or no. 2) containing the error.
2. Also indicate the voice where the error occurs:
   S = Soprano   A = Alto   T = Tenor   B = Bass

The example indicates the correct procedure.

Chord: 2   ___ ___ ___ ___ ___ ___

Voice: A   ___ ___ ___ ___ ___ ___

Harmony 10C

Harmonic Dictation: Dominant 7th
Chord in Four-Part Chorale Phrases

Each exercise consists of a chorale phrase.

Numbers	No. of Chords	Position
1–6	4	All in root position
7–12	7	Root position and inversions

1. Indicate the Roman numeral analysis of each triad in the blanks provided.
2. List any nonharmonic tones beneath the harmonic analysis.
3. If the instructor requests it, give the melodic line of both the soprano and bass voices.
4. If the instructor requests it, give the melodic line of both the alto and tenor voices.

1. CM: I ___ ___ ___

2. D m: i ___ ___ ___

3. D M: I ___ ___ ___

4. E♭ M: iii ___ ___ ___

5. E m: i ___ ___ ___

6. A M: vi ___ ___ ___

7. CM: I ___ ___ ___ ___ ___ ___
   UPT

8. B♭ M: I ___ ___ ___ ___ ___ ___
   UPT

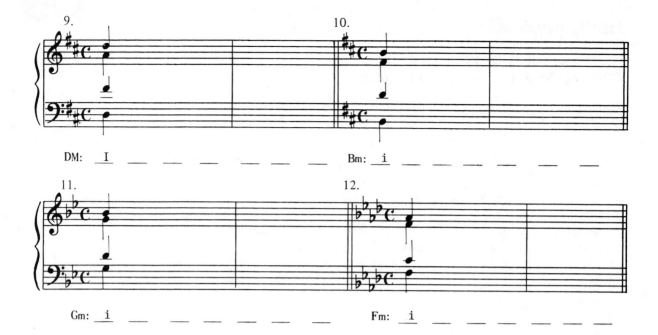

DM: I _ _ _ _ _ _   Bm: i _ _ _ _ _ _

Gm: i _ _ _ _ _ _   Fm: i _ _ _ _ _ _

Harmony 10D

Identifying Harmonic and Melodic Relationships in Musical Periods from Haydn Sonatas

Each exercise consists of a period (two phrases) extracted from a Haydn piano sonata.

Using the measure and beat numbers provided, complete the following:

1. Bracket the harmonic rhythm beneath the numbers.
2. Under each bracket indicate the chord analysis. The instructor will indicate which of the following is preferred:
   a. Write only the basic chords—it is not necessary to show inversions.
   b. Write the basic chords and include the proper inversion. Use the lowest sounding tone within each bracket in determining the position of the chord.
3. Bracket the phrases above the numbers.
4. At the end of each phrase bracket, indicate the type of cadence.

1. 3/4 meter with upbeat. Large numbers denote the first beat of the measure.

BEATS: 1   **2**   3   4   **5**   6   7   **8**   9   10   **11**   12   13

        14   15   16   **17**   18   19   **20**   21   22   **23**   24

2. 3/8 meter with upbeat. Large numbers denote the first beat of the measure.

BEATS: 1   2   3   4   5   6   7   8   9   10   11   12   13

14   15   16   17   18   19   20   21   22   23   24   25

(R) 3. 3/4 meter. Large numbers denote the first beat of the measure.

BEATS: 1   2   3   4   5   6   7   8   9   10   11   12   13

14   15   16   17   18   19   20   21   22

(R) 4. 2/2 meter beat in 4 (with upbeat). Large numbers denote the first beat of the measures.

BEATS: 1   2   3   4   5   6   7   8   9

10   11   12   13   14   15   16   17   18   19   20   21

22   23   24   25   26   27   28   29   30

(R) 5. 2/4 meter. Large numbers denote the first beat of the measures.

BEATS: <u>1</u> 2 <u>3</u> 4 <u>5</u> 6 <u>7</u> 8 <u>9</u> 10 <u>11</u> 12 <u>13</u>

14 <u>15</u> 16

(R) 6. 2/4 meter with upbeat. Large numbers denote the first beat of the measures.

BEATS: UP <u>1</u> 2 <u>3</u> 4 <u>5</u> 6 <u>7</u> 8 <u>9</u> 10 <u>11</u> 12

<u>13</u> 14 <u>15</u> 16 <u>17</u> 18 <u>19</u> 20 <u>21</u> 22 <u>23</u> 24

<u>25</u> 26 <u>27</u> 28 <u>29</u> 30 <u>31</u> 32 <u>33</u> 34 <u>35</u> 36

Rhythm 10A

Rhythmic Dictation: Triple and Triplet Subdivisions

Each exercise consists of a short melodic excerpt of music. Most, but not all of these exercises contain triple or triplet subdivision of the beat.

Complete the rhythm of each excerpt on a neutral pitch.

1.

2.

3.

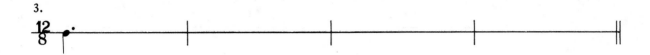

4.

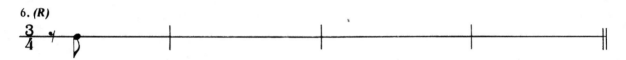

5. *(R)*

These rhythms are a review of previous material.

6. *(R)*

7. *(R)*

8. *(R)*

Rhythm 10B

Rhythmic Dictation: Two-Voiced Rhythms

Each exercise consists of a two-voiced excerpt.

Complete the rhythmic values for both voices on a neutral pitch.

1.

2.

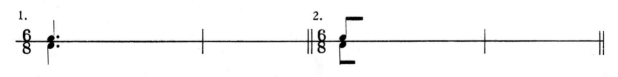

3.

4.

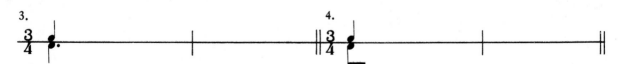

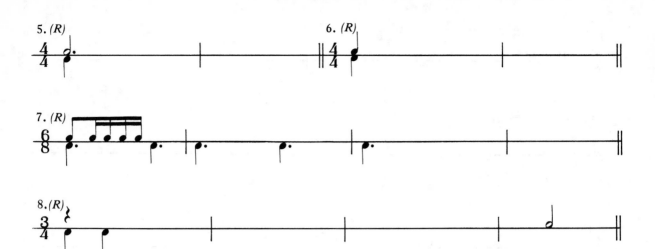

UNIT 11

Melody 11A

Melodic Dictation: Modulation to Closely Related Keys

Each exercise consists of a melodic excerpt that modulates to a closely related key.

Complete the melody on the staff in notation.

*(R) means recorded.

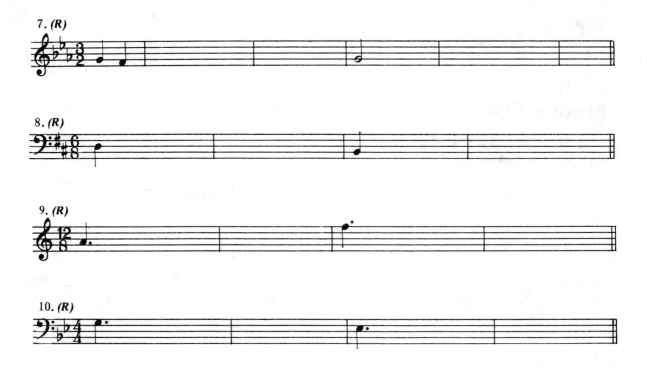

Melody 11B

Melodic Dictation: Themes from Music Literature Lacking Accidentals

Each exercise consists of a short melodic excerpt from music literature.

1. The following themes are excerpted from the interior of longer compositions, and the actual key of the melody is in conflict with the key signature.
2. In your printed version, the accidentals that would help to determine the actual key of the excerpts have been removed.

   The instructor plays the excerpt exactly as written by the composer.

3. Write the missing accidentals on the staff in notation.
4. Write the key of the melody in the blank provided.

The notes of each melody are numbered for convenience in class discussions.

2.

Actual key of melody: _____

1   2   3   4   5   6   7 8 9   10   11   12   13   14   15   16 17

3.

Actual key of melody: _____

1 2   3   4   5   6   7   8   9   10 11 12 13 14   15 16 17 18 19 20   21

4.

Actual key of melody: _____

1   2   3   4 5   6   7   8   9 10 10½ 11   12 13   14 15   16   17 18

5.

Actual key of melody: _____

1   2 3 4 5 6   7   8   9   10 11   12   13   14   15 16 17 18 19 20   21

6. (R)

Actual key of melody: _____

1   2   3   4   5   6   7   8   9   10 11 12 13 14 15   16

7. (R)

Actual key of melody: _____

1   2   3   4   5   6   7   8   9   10   11 12   13 14   15 16   17 18   19 20   21 22   23 24 25 26 27

8. (R)

Actual key of melody: _____

1   2   3   4   5   6   7   8   9   10   11   12   13   14   15   16   17   18

9. *(R)*

Actual key of melody: _____

10. *(R)*

Actual key of melody: _____

Melody 11C

Melodic Dictation: Two Voices

Each exercise consists of a short excerpt of music in two voices.

1. Numbers 1–10: Write the numbers indicating the harmonic intervals occurring between the two voices. It is not necessary to give the quality of the interval. Thus, instead of P 8, M 3, A 4, M 7, and so on, simply state 8, 3, 4, 7, and so on.
2. Numbers 11–16: Complete the two-voiced compositions as dictated. The first note in each voice is given.

1. ___ ___ ___ ___ ___ ___ ___
   1   2   3   4   5   6   7

2. ___ ___ ___ ___ ___ ___ ___ ___ ___ ___
   1   2   3   4   5   6   7   8   9   10

3. ___ ___ ___ ___ ___ ___ ___ ___ ___ ___
   1   2   3   4   5   6   7   8   9   10

4. ___ ___ ___ ___ ___ ___ ___ ___ ___ ___
   1   2   3   4   5   6   7   8   9   10

5. ___ ___ ___ ___ ___ ___ ___ ___
   1   2   3   4   5   6   7   8

6. ___ ___ ___ ___ ___ ___ ___
   1   2   3   4   5   6   7

7. ___ ___ ___ ___ ___ ___ ___
   1   2   3   4   5   6   7

8. ___ ___ ___ ___ ___ ___ ___ ___
   1   2   3   4   5   6   7   8

(R) 9. ___ ___ ___ ___ ___ ___ ___
   1   2   3   4   5   6   7

(R)10.

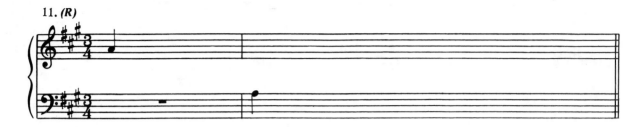

11. (R)

12. (R)

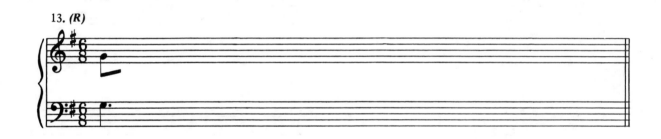

13. (R)

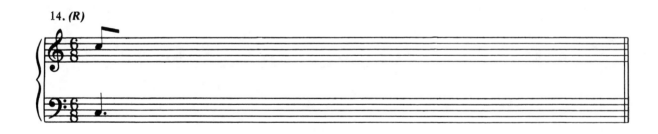

14. (R)

15. (R)

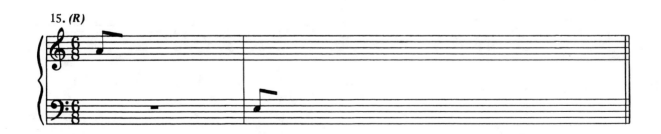

16. (R)

Melody 11D

Intervals: All Intervals
Played Harmonically

Each exercise consists of a single interval played harmonically.

1. Write the name of the interval in the blank provided.
2. Write the remaining note on the staff.

The given note is the lower of the two:

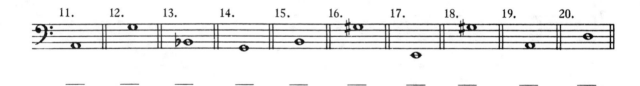

The given note is the upper of the two:

31.–60. (R)

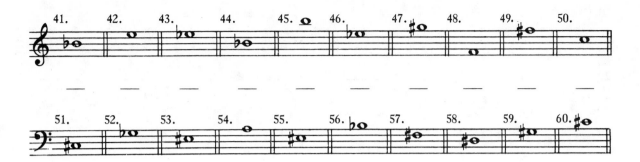

Harmony 11A

Chord Identification: vii°⁷
(Diminished 7th Chord) and Inversions

Each exercise consists of a series of four chords in block harmony.

Indicate the analysis of each of the four chords in the blank provided.

The new chord:

E minor: vii°⁷

Numbers 1–15 contain root-position chords only:

(R) 1. _____ _____ _____ _____   (R) 9. _____ _____ _____ _____

(R) 2. _____ _____ _____ _____   (R)10. _____ _____ _____ _____

(R) 3. _____ _____ _____ _____   11. _____ _____ _____ _____

(R) 4. _____ _____ _____ _____   12. _____ _____ _____ _____

(R) 5. _____ _____ _____ _____   13. _____ _____ _____ _____

(R) 6. _____ _____ _____ _____   14. _____ _____ _____ _____

(R) 7. _____ _____ _____ _____   15. _____ _____ _____ _____

(R) 8. _____ _____ _____ _____

Numbers 16–25 contain inversions:

16. _____ _____ _____ _____   18. _____ _____ _____ _____

17. _____ _____ _____ _____   19. _____ _____ _____ _____

20. _____ _____ _____ _____ 23. _____ _____ _____ _____

21. _____ _____ _____ _____ 24. _____ _____ _____ _____

22. _____ _____ _____ _____ 25. _____ _____ _____ _____

Harmony 11B

Harmonic Dictation: Four-Part Chorale
Phrases That Modulate

Each exercise consists of a chorale phrase.

Numbers	No. of Chords	Position	Nonharmonic Tones
1–9	5	Root position only	Occasional passing tone
10–16	7–9	Root position and inversions	Several—any type

For numbers 1–9 (practice outside of class):

1. Identifying modulations is not easy and requires some long range thinking. Numbers 1–9 afford an ideal introduction because in each phrase:

Chord No.	Function
1	Is always tonic in the original key
1–3	Always establishes the original key.
5	Is always tonic in the new key
4–5	Always forms a cadence in the new key.

This narrows the possibilities and gives you an opportunity to concentrate on the modulation itself. The following procedure is recommended:

2. Practice recognition of inversions in numbers 10–16.
3. Listen to all five chords. Compare the first and last chords. Remember that both are tonic chords—original and new.
4. Sing only the roots of the two chords—first, then second. You can tell the relationship of the two by the interval formed.
5. When you have figured out the new key, analyzing the five chords is considerably simplified.
6. Indicate Roman numeral analysis of each triad. Because all phrases modulate the blanks have been omitted throughout.
7. List any nonharmonic tones beneath the harmonic analysis.
8. If the instructor requests it, give the melodic line of both the soprano and bass voices.
9. If the instructor requests it, give the melodic line of both the alto and tenor voices.

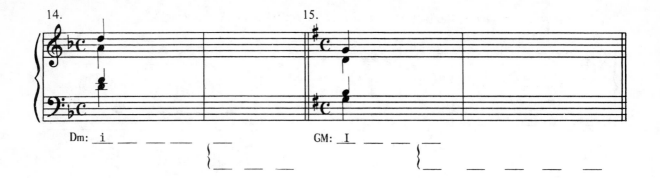

14.

15.

Dm: i ___ ___ ___ ___

GM: I ___ ___ ___

Harmony 11C

Key, Phrase, and Cadence Relationships

Each exercise consists of four phrases of music by Baroque composers.

Listen carefully three or four times to each excerpt and then answer the multiple choice questions. Each question has only one correct answer. Circle the letter indicating the correct answer.

The instructor now plays no. 1. (R)

Assume that this excerpt contains four phrases. It begins in B-flat major.

1. Keys expressed in this excerpt are:

    A.   B♭M,   FM,   and E♭M

    B.   B♭M,   Cm,   and FM

    C.   B♭M,   E♭M,   only

    D.   B♭M,   E♭M,   and FM

    E.   B♭M,   FM,   only

2. The relationship of the four phrases in this excerpt is:

    A   A'   A'   A   B

    B.   A   B   A   C

    C.   A   B   A'   C

    D.   A   B   A   B

    E.   A   A'   A   A

3. The cadence punctuating the four phrases of this excerpt (in order of appearance):

    A. authentic, half, authentic, half

    B. half, authentic, half, authentic

    C. all are authentic

    D. authentic, authentic, half, authentic

    E. deceptive, authentic, half, authentic

4. Harmony in the first phrase (in order of appearance) is:

    A. tonic to dominant to tonic

    B. tonic to subdominant to dominant to tonic

    C. tonic to dominant

    D. tonic to supertonic to dominant to tonic

    E. tonic to subdominant to dominant

The instructor now plays no. 2. (R)

Assume that this excerpt contains four phrases. The composition begins in G minor.

5. The cadences at the end of the 2nd and 4th phrases are (in order of appearance):

    A. authentic, authentic

    B. authentic, half

    C. half, authentic

    D. plagal, half

    E. half, half

6. The phrase relationships are:

    A. A   B   B′   C

    B. A   B   A′   C

    C. A   B   A   B

    D. A   A′   B   C

    E. A   A′   A′   B

7. The excerpt begins in G minor and ends in:

   A. B-flat minor

   B. E-flat minor

   C. C minor

   D. D minor

   E. A minor

The instructor now plays no. 3. (R)

Assume this excerpt contains four phrases. It begins in F major.

8. The keys in order of their appearance are:

   A.   FM   B♭M   CM   FM

   B.   FM   GM   B♭M   FM

   C.   FM   CM   GM   FM

   D.   FM   DM   CM   FM

   E.   FM   CM   B♭M   FM

9. The phrase relationships are:

   A.   A   A′   A″   C

   B.   A   A′   B   A

   C.   A   B   A   B′

   D.   A   B   A′   C

   E.   A   B   B   C

10. The cadences (punctuating the phrases) in order of appearance are:

    A. half, authentic, half, authentic

    B. all are authentic cadences

    C. plagal, authentic, plagal, authentic

    D. half, half, half, authentic

    E. authentic, half, half, authentic

Harmony 11D

Harmonic Dictation: Modulations
to Closely Related Keys

Each exercise consists of a phrase from a Bach chorale that modulates.

1. Indicate the analysis of each chord beneath the lower staff.
2. List nonharmonic tones beneath the harmonic analysis.
3. Write the melodic line of both the soprano and bass voices.
4. Write the melodic line of both the alto and tenor voices.

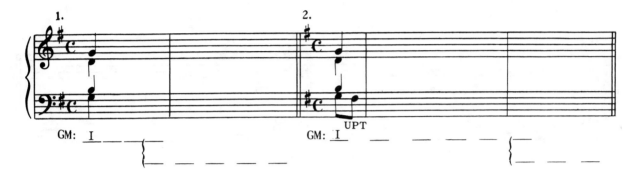

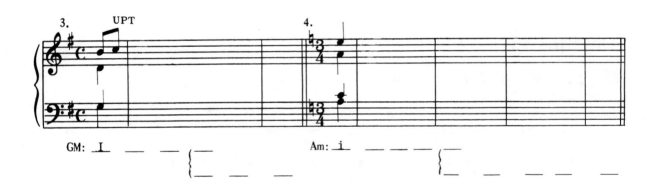

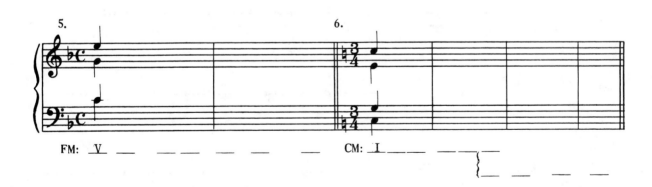

CM: I _ _ _   {_ _ _ _ _ _ _

FM: I _ _ _   {_ _ _ _ _ _ _

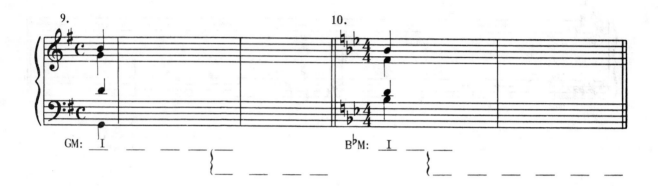

GM: I _ _ _ _   {_ _ _ _ _ _

B♭M: I _ _   {_ _ _ _ _ _

Rhythm 11A

Error Detection: More Difficult
Errors in Rhythm

Each exercise consists of a short melody with one rhythmic error.

Circle the number indicating the beat that differs rhythmically from what is written.

Rhythm 11B

Rhythmic Dictation: The Quartolet

Each exercise consists of a short rhythmic excerpt. Many, but not all of these exercises contain **quartolets,** rhythmic groupings of four normally given to groupings of three.

Complete the rhythm on a neutral pitch.

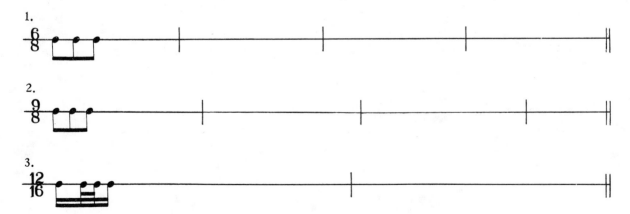

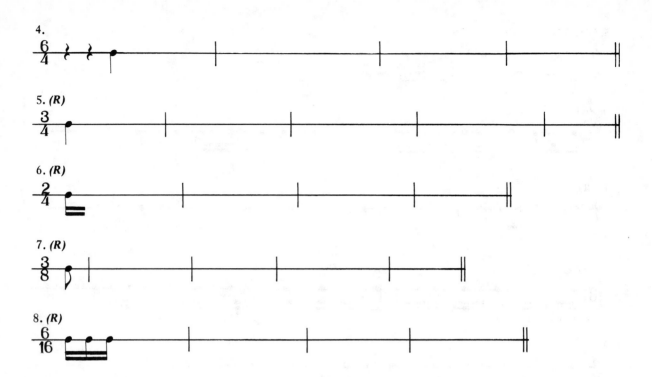

UNIT 12

Melody 12A

Melodic Dictation: Modulation in Two-Phrase Periods

Each exercise is a melody composed of two phrases. The second phrase begins immediately after the ‖, marked in each melody, and ends with a modulation.

1. Complete each melody on the staff in notation. The first note(s) of each phrase is given. In all periods the second phrase ends on the new tonic.
2. As you hear the melody, try to memorize each phrase so that you can sing it accurately in your mind.
3. Think of the scale degree each pitch represents by including solfeggio syllables or numbers.
4. When all pitches are accounted for, you are ready to write the phrase on the staff.

*(R) means recorded.

Melody 12B

Error Detection: Excerpts
from Music Literature

Each exercise consists of a short melodic excerpt from music literature.

1. In each exercise, the notes are on the proper lines or spaces, but either lack proper accidentals or contain accidentals that should be removed. The first note of each exercise is correct.
2. Add or delete accidentals to make the printed copy conform to that played by the instructor. Do not change the spelling of the notes.
3. The notes in each exercise are numbered for convenience in class discussions.

3.

4.

5.

6. (R)

7. (R)

8. (R)

9. (R)

10. (R)

Melody 12C

Melodic Dictation: Intervals—Two in Succession

Each exercise consists of three tones played melodically. The first note is given.

Write the two remaining notes on the staff.

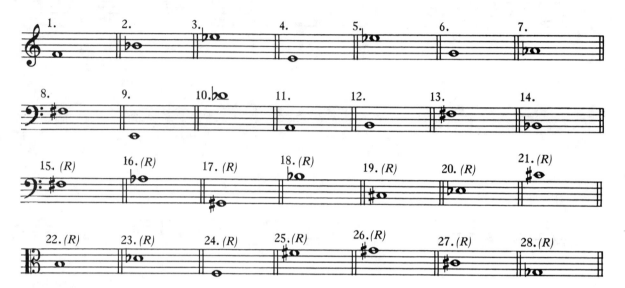

Harmony 12A

Chord Identification: Nondominant 7th Chords

Each exercise consists of a series of four chords in block harmony.

1. Indicate the analysis of the four chords in the blanks provided.
2. Numbers 1–15 are in root-position only:

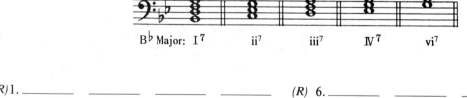

B♭ Major: I⁷   ii⁷   iii⁷   IV⁷   vi⁷

(R)1. _____ _____ _____ _____   (R) 6. _____ _____ _____ _____

(R)2. _____ _____ _____ _____   (R) 7. _____ _____ _____ _____

(R)3. _____ _____ _____ _____   (R) 8. _____ _____ _____ _____

(R)4. _____ _____ _____ _____   (R) 9. _____ _____ _____ _____

(R)5. _____ _____ _____ _____   (R)10. _____ _____ _____ _____

11. _____ _____ _____ _____   14. _____ _____ _____ _____

12. _____ _____ _____ _____   15. _____ _____ _____ _____

13. _____ _____ _____ _____

3. Numbers 16–25 contain inversions:

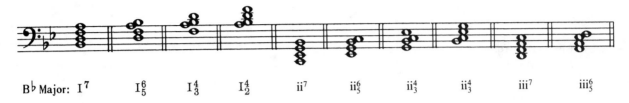

B♭ Major: I^7 I^6_5 I^4_3 I^4_2 ii^7 ii^6_5 ii^4_3 ii^4_3 iii^7 iii^6_5

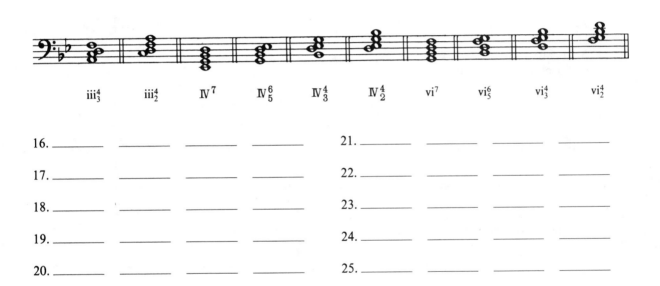

iii^4_3 iii^4_2 IV^7 IV^6_5 IV^4_3 IV^4_2 vi^7 vi^6_5 vi^4_3 vi^4_2

16. _____ _____ _____ _____   21. _____ _____ _____ _____

17. _____ _____ _____ _____   22. _____ _____ _____ _____

18. _____ _____ _____ _____   23. _____ _____ _____ _____

19. _____ _____ _____ _____   24. _____ _____ _____ _____

20. _____ _____ _____ _____   25. _____ _____ _____ _____

Harmony 12B

Identifying Modulations to Closely Related and Foreign Keys

Each exercise consists of a series of seven chords beginning in C major and modulating to a closely related or foreign key.

1. In the blank provided, write the name of the key to which the phrase modulates. All begin in the key of C.
2. The instructor may ask some class members to provide a harmonic analysis of each chord in the excerpt. Blanks are provided for the purpose.
   1. Modulates from C major to _____ .
      Optional harmonic analysis:

_____ _____ _____ _____ _____ _____ _____

2. Modulates from C major to _____ .
Optional harmonic analysis:

_____ _____ _____ _____   _____ _____ _____

3. Modulates from C major to _____ .
Optional harmonic analysis:

_____ _____ _____ _____   _____ _____ _____

4. Modulates from C major to _____ .
Optional harmonic analysis:

_____ _____ _____ _____   _____ _____ _____

5. Modulates from C major to _____ .
Optional harmonic analysis:

_____ _____ _____ _____   _____ _____ _____

6. Modulates from C major to _____ .
Optional harmonic analysis:

_____ _____ _____ _____   _____ _____ _____

(R) 7. Modulates from C major to _____ .
Optional harmonic analysis:

_____ _____ _____ _____   _____ _____ _____

(R) 8. Modulates from C major to _____ .
Optional harmonic analysis:

_____ _____ _____ _____   _____ _____ _____

(R) 9. Modulates from C major to _____ .
Optional harmonic analysis:

_____ _____ _____ _____   _____ _____ _____

(R)10. Modulates from C major to _____ .
Optional harmonic analysis:

_____ _____ _____ _____   _____ _____ _____

(R)11. Modulates from C major to _____ .
Optional harmonic analysis:

_____ _____ _____ _____   _____ _____ _____

(R)12. Modulates from C major to _____ .
Optional harmonic analysis:

_____ _____ _____ _____   _____ _____ _____

Harmony 12C

Chord Identification: MM, Mm, mm, Dm, and dd 7th Chords

Each exercise consists of a single 7th chord.

1. In the blanks, write the abbreviation for the type of 7th chord played.

   MM = MAJOR TRIAD AND MAJOR 7TH

   Mm = MAJOR TRIAD AND MINOR 7TH

   mm = MINOR TRIAD AND MINOR 7TH

   Dm = DIMINISHED TRIAD AND MINOR 7TH

   dd = DIMINISHED TRIAD AND DIMINISHED 7TH

2. In numbers 1–20, all 7th chords are in root-position and the 7th is in the soprano (highest sounding) voice.

16.–30. (R)

1. _____	6. _____	11. _____	16. _____
2. _____	7. _____	12. _____	17. _____
3. _____	8. _____	13. _____	18. _____
4. _____	9. _____	14. _____	19. _____
5. _____	10. _____	15. _____	20. _____

3. In numbers 21–30, the 7th chords are all in root-position, but the 7th may be in any voice (except the bass, of course).

21. _____	24. _____	27. _____	30. _____
22. _____	25. _____	28. _____	
23. _____	26. _____	29. _____	

Harmony 12D

Analysis of a Four-Phrase Homophonic Excerpt

This section consists of a single four-phrase excerpt from a Beethoven piano sonata. *(R)*

1. Listen to the excerpt four to six times.
2. Become familiar with the statements that follow.
3. Circle the numbers representing *true* statements regarding the excerpt. The questions are grouped according to category.

PHRASE RELATIONSHIPS AND CONSTRUCTION

1. The first and third phrases are in modified repeated relationship (consider all voices).
2. The 2nd and 4th phrases are in contrasting relationship.
3. The 4th phrase contains a substantial phrase extension.
4. The 2nd phrase is parallel to the first.
5. The melody line (uppermost voice) of the first and third phrases contains a sequence.
6. The 3rd and 4th phrases are in modified repeated relationship.
7. The complete excerpt is a double period.

CADENCES

8. The only perfect authentic cadence occurs at the end of the excerpt.
9. The 2nd and 4th phrases end with different cadence types.
10. The 1st and 2nd cadences are of different types.

HARMONY AND NONHARMONIC TONES

11. The 1st phrase contains only tonic and dominant harmony.
12. The 2nd phrase contains only tonic and dominant harmony.
13. The excerpt modulates to the dominant.
14. The harmonic rhythm is consistently three chords only (two chord *changes*) per phrase.
15. The 1st phrase contains two prominent escape tones (uppermost voice).
16. The 1st phrase contains two appoggiaturas (in the uppermost voice).
17. The final cadence contains both a suspension and a retardation.

MISCELLANEOUS

18. The 3rd phrase contains an Alberti bass figure.
19. The complete excerpt contains an example of change of mode.
20. An ostinato figure the length of a phrase is heard throughout the excerpt (four times).

Harmony 12E

Error Detection: Triads and 7th Chords

Each exercise consists of two chords in four parts.

1. As played by the instructor, *one* note in each exercise is incorrect. Any voice may contain an error.
2. Indicate the chord (no. 1 or no. 2) containing the error.
3. Also indicate the voice where the error occurs:
   S = Soprano   A = Alto   T = Tenor   B = Bass

The example indicates the correct procedure.

Chord: __1__ ___ ___ ___ ___ ___ ___ ___ ___ ___
Voice: __B__ ___ ___ ___ ___ ___ ___ ___ ___ ___

Rhythm 12A

Rhythmic Dictation: 8th-Beat Values

Each excerpt consists of a short melodic excerpt.

Complete the rhythm on a neutral pitch.

1.

2.

3.

4.

5. *(R)*

6. *(R)*

7. *(R)*

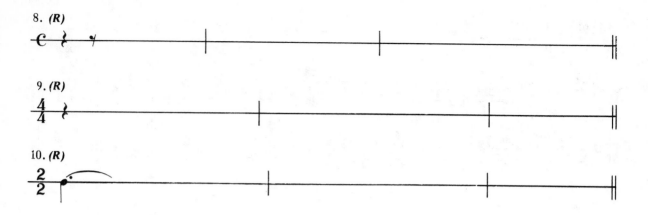

Rhythm 12B

Error Detection: 8th-Beat Values

Each exercise consists of a short melodic excerpt containing a single rhythmic error.

Circle the number indicating the point at which the printed version does not agree with that played.

UNIT 13

Melody 13A

Mode Identification: Dorian, Phrygian, Lydian, Mixolydian, and Aeolian Modes

Each exercise consists of the Dorian, Phrygian, Lydian, Mixolydian, or Aeolian scale.

See Melody 2C for information concerning these modes. The Aeolian mode is the same as the natural minor.

1. In the blank provided, name the mode you hear.

1. _____   6. _____

2. _____   7. _____

3. _____   8. _____

4. _____   9. _____

5. _____   10. _____

2. Numbers 11–20 consist of very short melodies utilizing the same modal scales played in numbers 1–10.
3. Write the name of the mode used in each melody.
4. The instructor may also ask you to write the key signature for each melody—the beginning tone, which is also the mode *final,* is given.

MODE:	BEGINNING TONE:	MODAL SIGNATURE (Number of sharps or flats in signature):
(R)*11. _____	D	_____
(R) 12. _____	A	_____
(R) 13. _____	C	_____
(R) 14. _____	A	_____
(R) 15. _____	A	_____
(R) 16. _____	F	_____
(R) 17. _____	D	_____
(R) 18. _____	E-FLAT	_____

*(R) means recorded.

Melody 13B

Adding Proper Accidentals
to Modal Melodies

Each exercise consists of a ten-note modal melody.

1. The first and last notes are correctly written, but the accidentals have otherwise been removed.
2. Write: the proper accidentals for each modal melody (Do not change the letter names of any of the notes. They are correct.)
3. Write the name of the mode in the blank above each score.

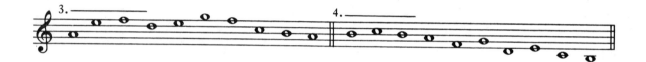

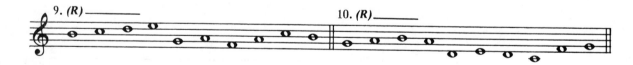

4. Exercises 11–15 are different from exercises 1–10 only in that they contain the element of rhythm.
5. The same directions apply to these as given for exercises 1–10.

Melody 13C

Melodic Dictation: Two-Voiced Modal Compositions

Each exercise consists of a short excerpt from a two-voiced composition of the sixteenth century.

Complete the melodies on the staff in notation.

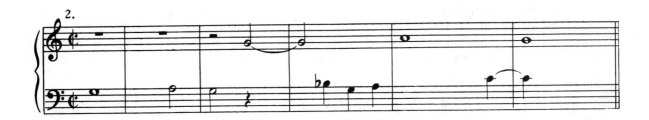

Melody 13D

Error Detection: Five-Note
Melodic Figures

Each exercise consists of a series of five tones with one pitch printed incorrectly. The first pitch (not lettered) is always correct.

Circle the letter (a, b, c, d) representing the incorrect pitch.

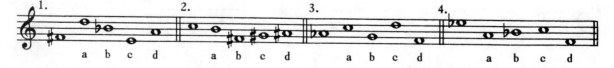

a b c d   a b c d   a b c d   a b c d   a b c d

10.–21. (R)

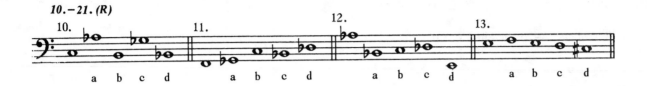

a b c d   a b c d   a b c d   a b c d

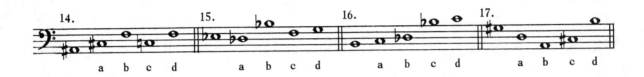

a b c d   a b c d   a b c d   a b c d

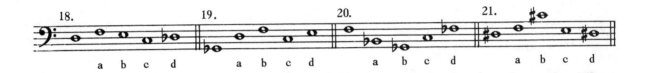

a b c d   a b c d   a b c d   a b c d

Harmony 13A

Chord Identification: Secondary Dominants of V and ii

Each exercise consists of a series of four chords in block harmony.

Analyze each of the four chords in the blanks provided.

New chords:

C Major: V/V   V⁷/V   vii°⁷/V   V/ii   V⁷/ii   vii°⁷/ii

Numbers 1–15 contain chords in root-position only.

(R)1. _____ _____ _____ _____   (R)5. _____ _____ _____ _____

(R)2. _____ _____ _____ _____   (R)6. _____ _____ _____ _____

(R)3. _____ _____ _____ _____   (R)7. _____ _____ _____ _____

(R)4. _____ _____ _____ _____   (R)8. _____ _____ _____ _____

(R) 9. _____ _____ _____ _____   13. _____ _____ _____ _____

(R)10. _____ _____ _____ _____   14. _____ _____ _____ _____

11. _____ _____ _____ _____   15. _____ _____ _____ _____

12. _____ _____ _____ _____

Numbers 16–25 contain inversions:

16. _____ _____ _____ _____   21. _____ _____ _____ _____

17. _____ _____ _____ _____   22. _____ _____ _____ _____

18. _____ _____ _____ _____   23. _____ _____ _____ _____

19. _____ _____ _____ _____   24. _____ _____ _____ _____

20. _____ _____ _____ _____   25. _____ _____ _____ _____

Harmony 13B

Harmonic Dictation: Four-Part Chorale Phrases Containing 7th Chords

Each exercise consists of a chorale phrase.

Numbers	No. of Chords	Position	Nonharmonic Tones
1–6	4	Root position only	Occasional passing tone
7–12	7–8	Root position and inversions	Several—any type

Suggested procedure for numbers 1–6: (Outside of class)

1. As you listen to each chord try to match the pitch of the root (bass pitch)—by *thinking* it rather than *singing* it.
2. Immediately recall the complete (four) succession of roots.
3. Associate the root pitchs with solfeggio syllables or numbers and write them down.
4. Convert the syllables or numbers to actual pitches and write out the bass notes on the staves provided.
5. If you wish, you can also add the basic analysis symbols too, but watch out for the presence of 7th chords, included in this assignment.
6. If your instructor requests, in successive listenings, pick out the soprano, alto, and tenor parts. Relate each to syllables or scale numbers.
7. Convert the syllables or numbers to actual pitches and add the notes to the staves.
8. When you have completed the phrase, listen one more time to check your answers.

1.

C M: I ___ ___ ___ ___

2.

E m: i ___ ___ ___ ___

3.

D M: I ___ ___ ___ ___

4.

F M: I ___ ___ ___ ___

5.

B♭ M: iii ___ ___ ___ ___

6.

G m: i ___ ___ ___ ___

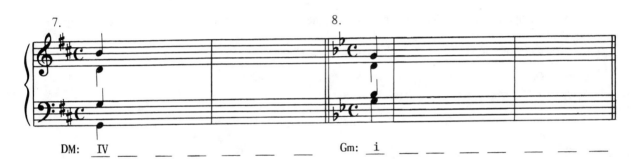

7.

DM: IV ___ ___ ___ ___

8.

Gm: i ___ ___ ___ ___

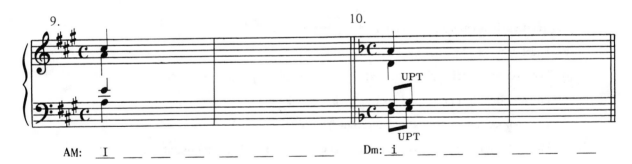

9.

AM: I ___ ___ ___ ___

10.

UPT

UPT

Dm: i ___ ___ ___ ___

11.

UPT

Bm: iv ___ ___ ___ ___

12.

F♯m: V⁶ ___

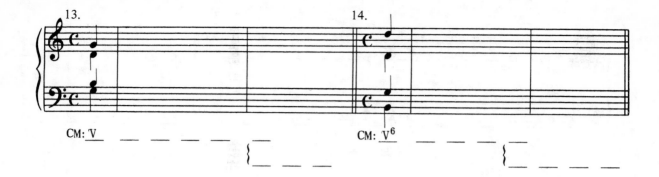

CM: V _ _ _ _ _   _

{ _ _ _

CM: V⁶ _ _ _ _

{ _ _ _ _

Harmony 13C

Phrase, Key, Cadence, and Harmonic Relationships in a Five-Phrase Homophonic Excerpt by Beethoven

The exercise consists of a single five-phrase excerpt from a Beethoven piano sonata. *(R)*

Listen to the five-phrase unit several times. Circle the *true* statements. Statements are grouped by subject matter.

1. Phrase relationships (only one of the five is correct):

   a.　A　　AP*　B　　A′　　C

   b.　A　　A　　B　　B′　　C

   c.　A　　AP　B　　A　　B′

   d.　A　　B　　C　　A′　　D

   e.　A　　B　　B′　　A′　　C

2. Key relationships (more than one may be correct):

   a. The 1st phrase does not modulate.

   b. The excerpt contains numerous (at least ten) secondary dominants.

   c. The 4th and 5th phrases are clearly in different keys.

   d. The composition ends in a key different from the beginning.

   e. The 2nd phrase ends with an authentic cadence in (or on) the dominant.

3. Cadences (more than one may be correct):

   a. Cadences at the ends of phrases represent authentic, half, and plagal types.

   b. The final cadence is authentic in the tonic key (key at the beginning of the excerpt).

   c. Most phrases of this excerpt can be divided into two-phrase members each with a cadence of its own.

   d. The 1st and 4th phrases end with different cadence types.

   e. The 1st cadence is decorated with a suspension.

*("P" refers to parallel phrase relationship)

Succession of chord roots contained in the first six chords of the final phrase of the excerpt (these will be played separately for you):

4. The succession of chord roots is (only one is correct):

a.	G	C	F	B♭	A♭	D♭
b.	G	C	B	E	D	G
c.	G	C	A	D	B	E
d.	G	E	A	D	G	C
e.	G	D	B	F#	D	A

Harmony 13D

Error Detection: Triads and 7th Chords

Each exercise consists of two chords in four parts.

1. As played by the instructor, one note in each exercise is incorrect. Errors may occur in the soprano, alto, or tenor voices.
2. Indicate the chord (no. 1 or no. 2) containing the error.
3. Also, indicate the voice where the error occurs:
   S = Soprano   A = Alto   T = Tenor

The example indicates the correct procedure.

Ex.
Chord: ____2____ ____ ____ ____ ____ ____ ____ ____ ____ ____

Voice: ____S____ ____ ____ ____ ____ ____ ____ ____ ____ ____

Rhythm 13A

Rhythmic Dictation: Introduction
to the Supertriplet

Each exercise consists of a short melodic excerpt.

Complete the rhythm on a neutral pitch. A **supertriplet** is a triplet that exceeds the length of a single beat.

Rhythm 13B

Error Detection

Each exercise consists of a melodic excerpt containing *one* error in rhythm.

Circle the number indicating the beat that is *not* played as notated.

UNIT 14

Melody 14A

Melodic Dictation: Two-Phrase Melodies

Each exercise is a melody composed of two phrases. The second phrase begins immediately after the ‖, marked in each melody. A variety of phrase, key, and cadential relationships exist in these examples from music literature.

1. Complete each melody on the staff in notation. The first note(s) of each phrase is given.
2. As you hear the melody, try to memorize each phrase so that you can sing it accurately in your mind.
3. Think of the scale degree each pitch represents by including solfeggio syllables or numbers.
4. When all pitches are accounted for, you are ready to write the phrase on the staff.
5. Be sure to notice relationships between the two phrases.

*(R) means recorded.

Melody 14B

Binary, Rounded Binary, and Three-Part Form

Each exercise consists of a complete composition in **binary, rounded binary, or three-part form.** Rounded binary lacks a truly distinct and independent B section and thus is distinguished from three-part form.

The measure numbers for each composition are given. The instructor will provide the beat duration so that you can follow the composition from the given numbers.

Indicate:

1. The phrases by bracketing the numbers (The first phrase of each composition is correctly bracketed for you.)
2. The phrase relationships:

      A   =   The first phrase of each composition or any other like it

      A′   =   Any other phrase that is a modified repetition of "A"

      AP =   A phrase that stands in parallel relationship to "A"

      B   =   A contrasting phrase to "A"

      B′   =   Any other phrase that is a modified repetition of "B"

3. The type of cadence at the end of each phrase
4. The key of each cadence
5. Any melodic sequences or repetitions (These are also given for the first phrase of each composition.)
6. The overall form of the composition

1. $\frac{2}{4}$ meter with upbeat. *(R)*

	┌─── Phrase A ───┐										
Measures: 1	2	3	4 No harmonic cadence	5	6	7	8	9	10	11	12
13	14	15	16	17	18	19	20	21	22	23	24

Overall Form: _____

2. $\frac{4}{4}$ meter. *(R)*

	┌─── Phrase A ───┐										
Measures: 1	2	3	4 Half C Major	5	6	7	8	9	10	11	12
13	14	15	16	17	18	19	20	21	22	23	24

Overall Form: _____

3. $\frac{3}{4}$ meter. *(R)*

	┌─── Phrase A ───┐								
Measures: 1	2	3	4 Authentic A Major	5	6	7	8	9	10
11	12	13	14	15	16	17	18	19	20
21	22	23	24	25	26	27	28	29	30
31	32	33	34	35	36	37	38	39	40
41	42	43	44	45	46	47	48	49	50
51	52	53	54	55	56	57	58		

Overall Form: _____

4. $\frac{3}{4}$ meter. *(R)*

Measures:	Phrase A									
	1 Rep	2 Rep	3	4 Authentic C Major	5	6	7	8	9	10
	11	12	13	14	15	16	17	18	19	20
	21	22	23	24	25	26	27	28			

Overall Form: _____

Melody 14C

Error Detection: Errors in Excerpts from Music Literature

Each exercise consists of a short melodic excerpt from compositions by Brahms containing three pitches that are played differently from those printed.

Circle the three numbers representing the pitches that differ from those played.

1.

2.

3.

4.

Melody 14D

Melodic Dictation: All Intervals—
Two and Three in Succession

Each exercise consists of two intervals (three tones) for exercises 1–10 and three intervals (four tones) for exercises 11–20.

1. Indicate the tones played in each exercise (The first note is given.)
2. Indicate the intervals produced in the blanks provided.

The example illustrates the correct procedure.

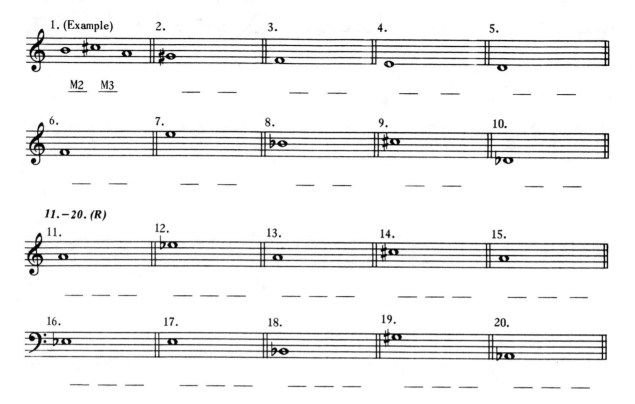

M2   M3

11.–20. (R)

Harmony 14A

Chord Identification: Secondary Dominants of IV or iv and vi or VI

Each exercise consists of a series of four chords in block harmony.

Indicate the analysis of each of the four chords in the blank provided.

New chords:

G Minor: V⁷/iv   vii°⁷/iv   V/VI   V⁷/VI   vii°⁷/VI

Numbers 1–15 contain root-position chords only:

(R) 1. _____ _____ _____ _____   (R) 4. _____ _____ _____ _____

(R) 2. _____ _____ _____ _____   (R) 5. _____ _____ _____ _____

(R) 3. _____ _____ _____ _____   (R) 6. _____ _____ _____ _____

(R) 7. _____ _____ _____ _____   12. _____ _____ _____ _____

(R) 8. _____ _____ _____ _____   13. _____ _____ _____ _____

(R) 9. _____ _____ _____ _____   14. _____ _____ _____ _____

(R) 10. _____ _____ _____ _____   15. _____ _____ _____ _____

11. _____ _____ _____ _____

Numbers 16–25 contain inversions:

16. _____ _____ _____ _____   21. _____ _____ _____ _____

17. _____ _____ _____ _____   22. _____ _____ _____ _____

18. _____ _____ _____ _____   23. _____ _____ _____ _____

19. _____ _____ _____ _____   24. _____ _____ _____ _____

20. _____ _____ _____ _____   25. _____ _____ _____ _____

Harmony 14B

Harmonic Dictation: Four-Part Chorale Phrases Containing Secondary Dominants

Each exercise consists of a chorale phrase.

Numbers	No. of Chords	Position	Nonharmonic Tones
1–6	4	Root position only	Occasional passing tone and suspension
7–12	7–9	Root position and inversions	Several—any type

For numbers 1–6 (practice outside of class):

It will help you to identify secondary dominants if you know the possibilities and common patterns. Numbers 1–6 contain no secondary leading tone chords or inversions, so you should concentrate on the following:

Major Triad or Dominant 7th Sounding 7th Chord on Scale Step:	Means a Secondary Dominant of:
1	IV
2	V
3	vi (VI in minor)
6	ii

1. As you listen to each chord try to match the pitch of the root (bass pitch) by *thinking* it rather than *singing* it.
2. Immediately recall the complete (four) succession of roots.
3. Associate the root pitches with solfeggio syllables or numbers.
4. Convert the syllables or numbers to actual pitches, and write out the bass notes on the staves provided.
5. Listen for major or major-minor sounds above each root—where you would normally expect minor triads and nondominant sounding 7th chords. In light pencil indicate these with a "V/" or "V7/." You can complete analysis later when you have more information.
6. If your instructor requests, in successive listenings pick out the soprano, alto, and tenor parts. Relate each to syllables or scale numbers.
7. Convert the syllables or numbers to actual pitches, and add the notes to the staves.
8. When you have completed the phrase, make sure you have placed the correct analysis symbols under those chords you determined to be secondary dominants (see step 5). Complete the analysis.

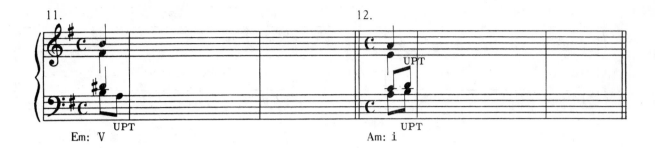

Em: V   Am: i

Harmony 14C

Harmonic Dictation: Modulation in Four-Part Chorale Phrases

Each exercise consists of a short chorale phrase that contains a modulation.

1. Write the analysis of each chord in the blank provided.
2. Write the soprano and bass melodies on the staff in notation.
3. Write the alto and tenor melodies on the staff in notation.

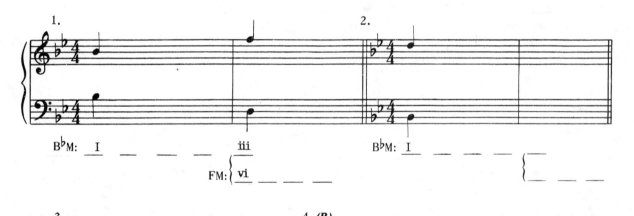

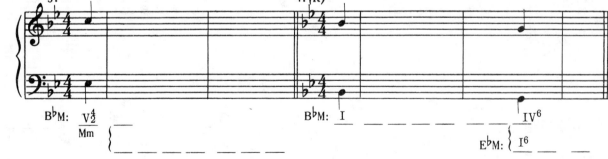

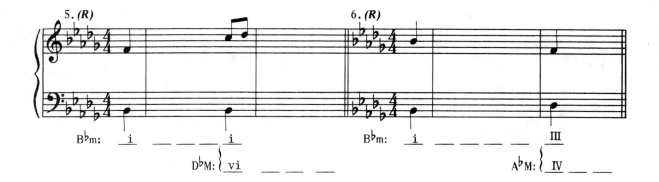

Harmony 14D

Error Detection: Triads and 7th Chords

Each exercise consists of three chords in four parts.

As played by the instructor, one note in each exercise is incorrect. Errors may occur in any voice.

1. Indicate the chord (no. 1, no. 2, or no. 3) containing the error.
2. Indicate the voice where the error occurs:
   S = Soprano   A = Alto   T = Tenor   B = Bass

The example illustrates the correct procedure.

Rhythm 14A

Rhythmic Dictation: Subtriplet in
Both Simple and Compound Meter

Each exercise consists of a short phrase of melody.

Complete the rhythm of each exercise on a neutral pitch.

1.

2.

3.

4.

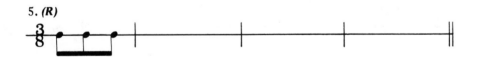

5. *(R)*

6. *(R)*

7. *(R)*

8. *(R)*

Rhythm Unit 14B

Error Detection: Rhythmic Errors

Each exercise consists of a short melodic phrase.

Circle the number indicating the beat that is *not* played as notated.

UNIT 15

Melody 15A

Melodic Dictation: Nondiatonic Tones

Each exercise consists of a short melodic excerpt containing one or two nondiatonic tones often suggesting secondary dominant harmony.

1. Listen to the melody. Determine the tonic—it is always the first pitch (given).
2. In your mind, construct the scale and sing or *think* it.
3. As you hear the melody again, memorize it in its entirety.
4. Be aware of one or two pitches that are nondiatonic.
5. When you have memorized the melody, sing it adding solfeggio syllables or numbers. Your instructor will tell you how to accommodate the nondiatonic pitches.
6. Convert the syllables or numbers to actual pitches, and notate the melody on the staff provided.

*(R) means recorded.

Melody 15B

Error Detection: Excerpts from Music Literature

Each exercise consists of a short melodic excerpt from music literature containing three pitches that are played differently from those printed.

Circle the numbers representing the pitches that are different from those played. There are *three* errors in each melody.

1.

2.

3.

4.

5.

6. (R)

Melody 15C

Melodic Dictation: Typical Blues Figures

Each exercise consists of two measures of melody characteristic of the blues.

BLUES   A black American song of lament supported by I, IV, and V harmony
                               and extending usually to twelve measures although eight, sixteen,
                               twenty-four, and thirty-two-bar blues are not uncommon.

BLUES SCALE   A major scale with an added flat 3rd and flat 7th.

These melodies may contain combinations of the natural 3rd, the flat 3rd, the natural 7th, and the flat 7th.
Although the following are only two measures long, they contain typical figures found in blues
compositions.

Complete each melody on the staff in notation.

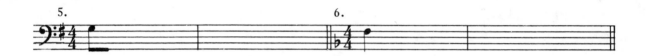

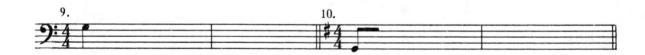

Melody 15D

Melodic Dictation: Four
Tones in Succession

Each exercise consists of four tones played in succession.

The first note is given. Write the remaining notes on the staff in notation.

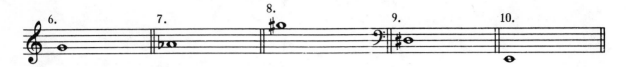

11.–20. (R)

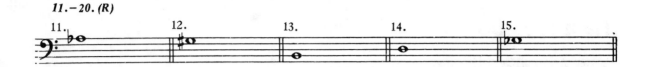

Harmony 15A

Chord Identification: All Secondary Dominants

Each exercise consists of a series of four chords in block harmony.

1. In the blank provided, analyze each of the four chords.
2. All of the secondary dominants studied to date plus that of iii are used. *All exercises are in G major.*

Numbers 1–15 contain root-position chords only.

(R) 1. _____ _____ _____ _____   (R) 9. _____ _____ _____ _____

(R) 2. _____ _____ _____ _____   (R) 10. _____ _____ _____ _____

(R) 3. _____ _____ _____ _____   11. _____ _____ _____ _____

(R) 4. _____ _____ _____ _____   12. _____ _____ _____ _____

(R) 5. _____ _____ _____ _____   13. _____ _____ _____ _____

(R) 6. _____ _____ _____ _____   14. _____ _____ _____ _____

(R) 7. _____ _____ _____ _____   15. _____ _____ _____ _____

(R) 8. _____ _____ _____ _____

Numbers 16–25 contain inversions.

16. _____ _____ _____ _____   18. _____ _____ _____ _____

17. _____ _____ _____ _____   19. _____ _____ _____ _____

20. _____ _____ _____ _____   23. _____ _____ _____ _____

21. _____ _____ _____ _____   24. _____ _____ _____ _____

22. _____ _____ _____ _____   25. _____ _____ _____ _____

Harmony 15B

Binary, Rounded Binary, and Three-Part Form

Each exercise consists of a complete composition in binary, rounded binary (incipient three-part), or three-part form.

The measure numbers for each composition are given. The instructor will count one measure before beginning to play so that you can follow the composition from the given numbers.

Indicate:

1. Bracket the phrases above the numbers (The first phrase of each composition is correctly bracketed.)
2. Indicate the phrase relationships above the brackets.
3. Indicate the type of cadence at the end of each phrase beneath the number.
4. Indicate the key of each cadence beneath the cadence type.
5. Bracket any melodic sequences or repetitions beneath the numbers.
6. Indicate the overall form of the composition (binary, rounded binary, or three-part form).

1. $\frac{2}{4}$ meter. Andante cantabile. *(R)*

	┌──── Phrase A ────┐								
Measures: 1	2	3	4	5	6	7	8	9	10
			Authentic C Major						
11	12	13	14	15	16	17	18	19	20
21	22	23	24	25	26	27	28	29	30
31	32	33	34	35	36	37	38	39	40

Overall Form: _____

2. $\frac{3}{2}$ meter. (R)

┌──────Phrase A──────┐

Measures: 1   2   3   4   5   6   7   8   9   10   11   12
                                    Half
                                    G minor

13   14   15   16   17   18   19   20   21   22

23   24   25   26   27   28   29   30   31   32

Overall Form: _____

3. $\frac{2}{2}$ meter with quarter note upbeat. (R)

┌──────Phrase A──────┐

Measures: 1   2   3   4   5   6   7   8   9   10   11
         └─Rep─┘└─Rep─┘   Authentic
                          D Major

12   13   14   15   16   17   18   19   20   21   22

Overall Form: _____

4. $\frac{6}{8}$ meter with eighth-note upbeat. (R)

┌──────Phrase A──────┐

Measures: 1   2   3   4   5   6   7   8   9   10
                                    Half
                                    A minor

11   12   13   14   15   16   17   18   19   20

21   22   23   24   25   26   27   28   29   30   31   32

Overall Form: _____

Rhythm 15A

Rhythmic Dictation: More Difficult Rhythms

Each exercise consists of a short melody.

Complete the rhythm on a neutral pitch.

1.

2.

3.

4.

5. (R)

6. (R)

7. (R)

8. (R)

Rhythm 15B

Error Detection: More Difficult

Each exercise consists of a short melodic excerpt containing one error in rhythm.

Circle the number indicating the rhythm that differs from that played.

UNIT 16

Melody 16A

Melodic Dictation: Nondiatonic Tones

Each exercise consists of a short melodic excerpt from music literature containing nondiatonic tones often suggesting momentary modulations or secondary dominant harmony.

1. Listen to the melody. The key is given above the staff. Figure the relationship of the first note to the tonic and sing it.
2. In your mind, construct the scale and sing or *think* it.
3. As you hear the melody again, memorize it in its entirety.
4. Be aware of some pitches that are nondiatonic.
5. When you have memorized the melody, sing it adding solfeggio syllables or numbers. Your instructor will tell you how to accommodate the nondiatonic pitches.
6. Convert the syllables or numbers to actual pitches, and notate the melody on the staff provided.

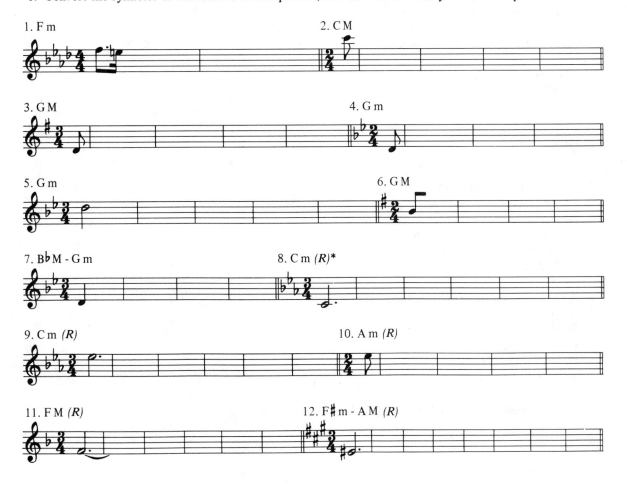

*(R) means recorded.

Melody 16B

Binary, Rounded Binary, and Three-Part Form

Each exercise consists of a complete composition in binary, rounded binary (incipient three-part), or three-part form.

Listen to Composition no. 1 two or three times; then, answer the following questions. Listen again to the composition to check your answers. *(R)*

1. The form is:
   A. three-part
   B. rounded binary
   C. rounded three-part
   D. incipient two-part
   E. two-part

2. This composition:
   A. modulates to the dominant and subdominant
   B. modulates to the dominant and relative minor
   C. modulates to the dominant only
   D. does not modulate
   E. modulates to the relative minor only

3. The number of phrases is:
   A. 2
   B. 6
   C. 4
   D. 3
   E. 7

4. Cadences represented are:
   A. plagal and authentic only
   B. authentic only
   C. deceptive, half, and authentic
   D. deceptive and authentic only
   E. half and authentic only

5. A phrase with a cadential extension is:
   A. the last
   B. the first
   C. the second
   D. does not occur
   E. both first and last

Listen to Composition no. 2 and answer the following questions: *(R)*

6. The form is:
   A. three-part
   B. rounded binary
   C. rounded three-part
   D. incipient two-part
   E. two-part

7. This composition:
   A. modulates to the dominant only
   B. modulates to the relative major only
   C. does not modulate
   D. modulates to the relative major and the dominant
   E. modulates to the relative major and subdominant

8. The cadence at the end of the first phrase is:
   A. authentic in the relative major
   B. authentic in the original key
   C. half in the original key
   D. plagal in the dominant key
   E. half in the relative major

The instructor will play an excerpt from composition no. 2.

9. This excerpt is an example of:
   1. repetition   A. 1, 2, 3, and 4
   2. a series of escape tones   B. 3 and 4 only
   3. sequence   C. 1, 3, and 4 only
   4. a succession of Mm7th chords   D. 2, 3, 4, and 5
   5. circle of 5ths progressions   E. 3, 4, and 5 only

10. This is an example of music from the:
    A. Baroque period
    B. Classical period
    C. Romantic period
    D. Renaissance period
    E. Post-Romantic period

Listen to Composition no. 3 and answer the following questions. (Note: The first phrase and some of the other phrases contain strong interior cadence-like figures.)*(R)*

11. The form is:
    A. three-part
    B. rounded binary
    C. rounded three-part
    D. incipient two-part
    E. two-part

12. The second phrase ends with a:
    A. deceptive cadence
    B. Phrygian cadence (iv^6-V)
    C. plagal cadence
    D. imperfect authentic cadence
    E. perfect authentic cadence

13. This composition basically contains:
    A. a through-composed melody
    B. phrases of uneven length
    C. parallel phrases combining to form periods
    D. sequences of phrase length
    E. an ostinato

14. Cadence types are:
    A. authentic, half, and plagal
    B. authentic only
    C. authentic, half, Phrygian, and deceptive
    D. authentic and plagal only
    E. authentic and Phrygian only

15. This is an example of music from the:
    A. Baroque period
    B. Classical period
    C. Romantic period
    D. Renaissance period
    E. Post-Romantic period

Melody 16C

Error Detection

Each exercise consists of a series of six pitches. One of the pitches is different from that played.

The first note of the series is always correct.

Circle the letter representing the pitch that is different from that played.

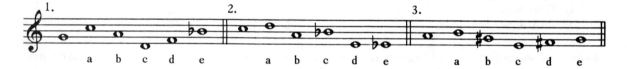

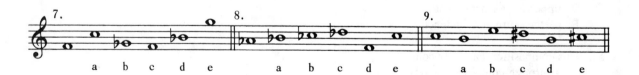

10. – 18. (R)

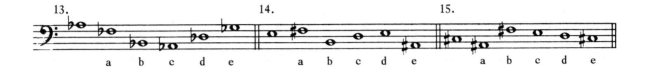

Harmony 16A

Chord Identification: German and French Augmented 6th Chords and the Neapolitan 6th Chord

Each exercise consists of four chords in four-part harmony.

Analyze each of the four chords in the blanks provided.

New chords:

G minor: Gr⁶   Fr⁶   N⁶

In these exercises the above chords are found in the positions shown:

Numbers 1–15 contain root-position chords only:

(R)1. _____ _____ _____ _____   (R)4. _____ _____ _____ _____

(R)2. _____ _____ _____ _____   (R)5. _____ _____ _____ _____

(R)3. _____ _____ _____ _____   (R)6. _____ _____ _____ _____

(R) 7. _____ _____ _____ _____   12. _____ _____ _____ _____

(R) 8. _____ _____ _____ _____   13. _____ _____ _____ _____

(R) 9. _____ _____ _____ _____   14. _____ _____ _____ _____

(R)10. _____ _____ _____ _____   15. _____ _____ _____ _____

11. _____ _____ _____ _____

Numbers 16–25 contain inversions:

16. _____ _____ _____ _____   21. _____ _____ _____ _____

17. _____ _____ _____ _____   22. _____ _____ _____ _____

18. _____ _____ _____ _____   23. _____ _____ _____ _____

19. _____ _____ _____ _____   24. _____ _____ _____ _____

20. _____ _____ _____ _____   25. _____ _____ _____ _____

Harmony 16B

Harmonic Dictation: Four-Part Chorale Phrases Containing Neapolitan and Augmented 6th Chords

Each exercise consists of a chorale phrase. Except for the Neapolitan (normally found in first inversion) and augmented 6th chords (bass note a major 3rd below the tonic), the content of the phrases is:

Numbers	No. of Chords	Position
1–4	7	Root position only
5–7	7–8	Root position and inversions

1. In numbers 1–4 the Neapolitan and augmented 6th chords are always treated in the most conventional manner.

   Neapolitan 6th chord

   1. Major triad whose root is a minor 2nd above the tonic.
   2. Bass note is the 4th scale degree.
   3. Proceeds to the V chord, sometimes through the tonic $^6_4$.

   Augmented 6th chords:

   1. Bass note is a major 3rd below the tonic.
   2. Italian and French types often proceed directly to V.
   3. German type will always progress to V but through the tonic 64.

4. Italian 6th sounds like a dominant 7th without its 5th factor.

5. French 6th does not sound like any diatonic chord, but it is a whole-tone chord—contains only whole steps (no half-steps).

2. The best way to identify the unique features of each augmented 6th chords is to play a number of them on the piano until you distinguish among the three types.

3. Numbers 5–7 contain root position and inversions.

4. Complete these phrases using the procedure in Melody 14B.

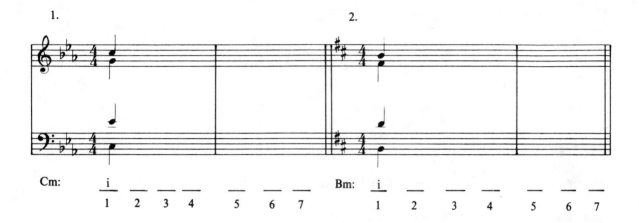

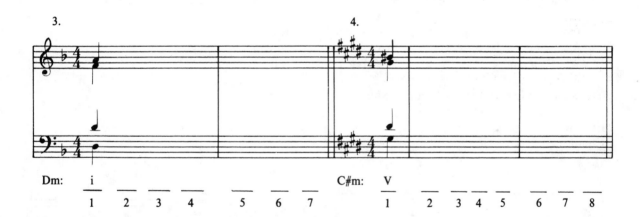

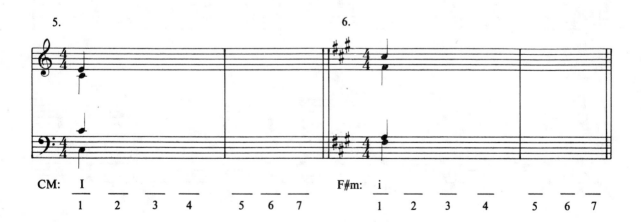

7.

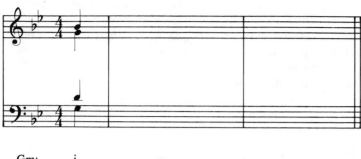

Gm: i
     ___ ___ ___ ___ ___ ___ ___ ___
      1   2   3   4   5   6   7   8

Harmony 16C

Error Detection: Triads and 7th Chords

Each exercise consists of three chords in four parts.

As played by the instructor, one note in each exercise is incorrect. Errors may occur in any voice.

1. Indicate the chord (no. 1, no. 2, or no. 3) containing the error.
2. Also, indicate the voice where the error occurs:
    S = Soprano   A = Alto   T = Tenor   B = Bass

The example illustrates the correct procedure.

Ex.
Chord: 2   ___ ___   ___ ___   ___ ___   ___ ___
Voice: A   ___ ___   ___ ___   ___ ___   ___ ___

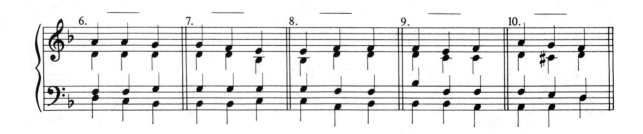

Harmony 16D

Chord Identification: MM, Mm,
mm, dm, and dd 7th Chords

Each exercise consists of a single 7th chord played in four-part harmony.

Only MM, Mm, mm, dm, and dd 7th chords are used.

In the blank, indicate the type of 7th chord played.

In numbers 1–10, all chords are in root-position and the 7th is in the soprano voice.

1. _____ _____ _____ _____   6. _____ _____ _____ _____

2. _____ _____ _____ _____   7. _____ _____ _____ _____

3. _____ _____ _____ _____   8. _____ _____ _____ _____

4. _____ _____ _____ _____   9. _____ _____ _____ _____

5. _____ _____ _____ _____   10. _____ _____ _____ _____

In numbers 11–20, all chords are in root position, but the 7th may be in any voice except the bass.

11. _____ _____ _____ _____   (R)16. _____ _____ _____ _____

12. _____ _____ _____ _____   (R)17. _____ _____ _____ _____

13. _____ _____ _____ _____   (R)18. _____ _____ _____ _____

14. _____ _____ _____ _____   (R)19. _____ _____ _____ _____

15. _____ _____ _____ _____   (R)20. _____ _____ _____ _____

In numbers 21–30, the chords may be in any position and the 7th in any voice.

(R)21. _____ _____ _____ _____   (R)26. _____ _____ _____ _____

(R)22. _____ _____ _____ _____   (R)27. _____ _____ _____ _____

(R)23. _____ _____ _____ _____   (R)28. _____ _____ _____ _____

(R)24. _____ _____ _____ _____   (R)29. _____ _____ _____ _____

(R)25. _____ _____ _____ _____   (R)30. _____ _____ _____ _____

Rhythm 16A

Rhythmic Dictation: Changing Meters

Each exercise consists of a short melody that employs changing meters.

Complete the rhythm on a neutral pitch, and complete any incomplete changing meters.

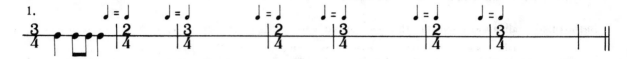

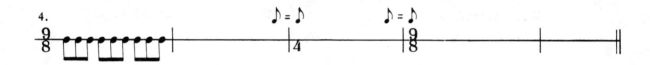

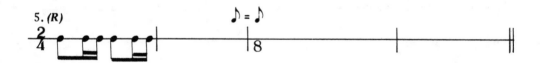

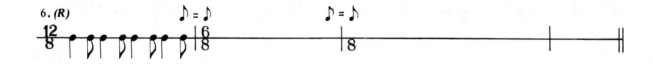

Rhythm 16B

Error Detection: Review

Each exercise consists of a short melodic excerpt containing one error in rhythm.

Circle the number indicating the beat that is *not* played as notated.

Index of Sections by Type

Melody

Harmony

P = Page   M1C = Melody 1C

Rhythm

Rhythmic Dictation			Errors in Rhythm	
P9	R1A		P34	R3A
P21	R2A		P49	R4A
P35	R3B		P62	R5B
P50	R4B		P75	R6B
P61	R5A		P101	R8B
P74	R6A		P142	R11A
P88	R7A		P154	R12B
P89	R7B		P165	R13B
P100	R8A		P178	R14B
P114	R9A		P187	R15B
P126	R10A		P199	R16B
P127	R10B (2 VOICE)			
P143	R11B			
P153	R12A			
P164	R13A			
P177	R14A			
P186	R15A			
P198	R16A			

Glossary

Accented neighboring tone	An accented nonharmonic tone that leads by step from one consonance (chord tone) to another of the same pitch. Example: c D c—where 'D' is the accented neighboring tone, while 'c' and 'c' are consonant chord tones. See notated example on page 20.
Accented passing tone	An accented nonharmonic tone that moves by step from one consonance (chord tone) to another of different pitch. Example: c D e—D is the accented passing tone, while 'c' and 'e' are the consonances (chord tones). See notated example on page 20.
Alberti bass	Figures of accompaniment, consisting generally of arpeggiations of a triad or 7th chord. First used in piano compositions to compensate for the quick sound decay associated with that instrument. Developed first by Domenico Alberti, the accompaniment figures later appeared in music for other instruments.
Anticipation	A nonharmonic (dissonant) tone that leads by step from a consonance (chord tone) to another by repetition. Example: g A a—where 'A' (dissonance) anticipates the pitch 'a', a chord tone in the next harmony. See notated example on page 19.
Appoggiatura	A nonharmonic (dissonant) tone preceded by a skip and resolved by step. Example: e A g#—where 'A' is the appoggiatura, leading by skip from a consonance 'e' and resolving down one scale step to 'g#'. See notated example on page 33.
Arpeggiated bass	A type of $^6_4$ chord which is part of an arpeggiated bass figure.
Arpeggiation	A term applied to the notes of a chord when they are played one after another instead of simultaneously.
Augmented triad	A three-tone chord consisting of two superimposed major 3rds. Example: C E G#.
Augmented 6th	A group of chords so named because they contain the interval of an augmented 6th. The bass note is usually a major 3rd below the tonic—in major or minor keys. Examples in the key of C major or minor:

$$\text{Italian} \quad = \quad A\flat \ C \ F\#$$

$$\text{German} \quad = \quad A\flat \ C \ E\flat \ F\#$$

$$\text{French} \quad = \quad A\flat \ C \ D \ F\#$$

For notated illustrations of augmented 6th chords see page 194.

Bass clef	The clef: 𝄢
Binary form	A two-part form with the two halves generally separated by a double bar. The first section often moves from tonic to dominant—or some other related key and ends with a cadence. The second section moves from dominant, relative major, or other related key back to the tonic. For a more thorough discussion see the Harvard Dictionary of Music.
Cadence	A melodic or harmonic formula providing a momentary or permanent conclusion. In this text the harmonic cadences are: Authentic (V-I or viio6-I), Plagal (IV-I), Half (I-V, ii-V, or IV-V), and Deceptive (V to vi).
Cadential	An adjective or adverb stemming from the word *cadence*.
Changing tones	Two successive nonharmonic (dissonant) tones. Leads by step from a chord tone (consonance), then skips to another nonharmonic tone, and finally resolves by step to a chord tone (consonance). Example: a B G# a—B and

G# are the changing tones (dissonant), and the 'a' on either end are chord tones. See notated example on page 33.

Chorale	A hymn tune (tune *only*) of the Protestant Church. The chorales were harmonized by a host of composers from the 17th through 20th centuries.
Chord	The simultaneous sounding of three or more pitches. In this text "chord" indicates a triad or 7th chord—three or four pitches arranged in major or minor 3rds and sounding together.
Chromatic scale	A twelve note scale identified by its exclusive use of half-step intervals. Example: C C# D D# E F F# G G# A A# B C.
Conjunct	Melodic movement by half or whole steps.
Consonance	Agreeable sounds. In this text the consonant intervals are: P unisons, 5ths, and octaves; and major and minor 3rds and 6ths. The P4th, while technically a consonance, is considered a dissonance for harmonic reasons.
Contrasting phrases	Two phrases, the second of which, although complementary to the first, has a different contour and makeup.
Deceptive cadence	A cadence progressing from dominant (V) to another that is not the tonic. V–vi is the most common.
Diatonic	Note or notes that are the pitches of a prescribed scale. In C major the diatonic pitches are: C D E F G A B.
Diminished triad	A three-tone chord consisting of two superimposed minor thirds. Example: B D F.
Disjunct	Melodic movement by intervals larger than a whole step.
Dissonance	Disagreeable sounds. In this text the dissonant intervals are: P4th, major and minor 2nds and 7ths, and all diminished and augmented intervals. The P4th, while technically a consonance, is considered a dissonance for harmonic reasons.
Dominant	Fifth scale step.
Dorian mode	A system of seven tones with the same arrangement as from D to D on the white keys of the piano.
Escape tone	A nonharmonic (dissonant) tone that leads by step from a chord tone (consonance), then skips to another of different pitch. Example: g A f— where "A" is the escape tone leading from consonance "g," and then skips down a M3rd to another consonance "f." See notated example on page 19.
False sequence	A melodic excerpt consisting partly of a sequence and partly of repetition. Example: C d e C e f C f g—where de, ef, and fg form a sequence, and C C C comprises a repetition. See a notated example on page 40.
Half cadence	A cadence ending on the dominant (V) harmony. Most often found as IV–V, ii–V or I–V.
Harmonic minor scale	A minor scale identified by half-step intervals between scale steps 2–3, 5–6, and 7–8. See notated example on page 1.
Homophonic	Music with a texture consisting of one voice that stands out melodically, supported by a chordal accompaniment either simple or elaborated.
Imperfect authentic	An authentic cadence (V to I) in which: (1) the highest sounding tone in the final chord is *not* the tonic pitch. (2) the dominant or tonic chord is *not* in root position, or (3) the leading tone triad (viio) or 7th chord is substituted for the dominant (V).
Interval	The difference (in vibrations) between two pitches.
Inversions	Refers, in this text, to triads or 7th chords in which the lowest sounding tone is *not* the root of the chord.
Leading tone	7th scale step of major, melodic, and harmonic minor scales. The 7th step of the natural minor scale is called the subtonic because that pitch is more than a half-step from the tonic.

Lydian mode	A system of seven tones with the same arrangement as from F to F on the white keys of the piano.
Major triad	A three-tone chord built on a superimposed major then minor third. Example: C E G.
Major scale	A seven-tone scale with half-steps between scale steps 3–4 and 7–8.
Mediant	Third scale step.
Melody	An organized succession of pitches.
Melodic minor scale	An ascending minor scale distinguished by the placement of half-steps at scale steps 2–3 and 7–8. The descending form of the melodic minor is the same as the natural minor.
Meter	The system of regularly recurring pulses most often grouped by periodic accents. Example: $\frac{3}{4}$ meter indicates that the beats are grouped by three's with the quarter note representing one beat or pulse.
Minor triad	A three-tone chord built on a superimposed minor then major third. Example: A C E.
Mixolydian mode	A system of seven tones with the same arrangements as from G to G on the white keys of the piano.
Modes	In this text, the word *mode* refers to the church modes (also known as Gregorian modes or Ecclesiastical modes).

Dorian: D E F G A B C D   Phrygian: E F G A B C D E
Lydian: F G A B C D E F   Mixolydian: G A B C D E F G
Aeolian: A B C D E F G A   Ionian: C D E F G A B C

See notated examples of the modes on pages 13 and 155.

Modal signature	While the modes are often explained as segments of the white keys of the piano, they were, in music literature, often transposed—in the same manner as the later major and minor scales of the 17th and 18th centuries. Modal signatures (similar to those in tonal music) are used for the transposed modes.
Neapolitan sixth chord	An altered chord consisting of a major triad on the lowered second scale degree. The Neapolitan 6th chord is found more often in minor than in major keys. The "6th" is appended to indicate that the chord most often occurs in first inversion.
Neighboring tone	A nonharmonic tone that leads by step from one chord tone to another of the same pitch. Neighboring tones may occur as accented or unaccented. Example: c D c—where "D" is the neighboring tone. For a notated illustration, see page 19.
Nonharmonic tone	Not harmonic—not a chord tone. A pitch, sounding along with a chord, but not a note of the chord. Some types of nonharmonic tones are: passing tone, neighboring tone, suspension, anticipation, escape tone, appoggiatura, pedal tone, changing tones. For notated illustrations of nonharmonic tones, see pages 19–20.
Parallel phrases	Two adjacent phrases (often comprising a period) where the beginning portion of both phrases is essentially the same, but the first ends with a half cadence, while the second is completed with an authentic cadence.
Passing bass	A type of $\frac{6}{4}$ usage where the lowest sounding tone of the $\frac{6}{4}$ chord acts as a passing tone.
Pedal point	A nonharmonic tone that is held or repeated, usually in the lowest voice, and alternates between consonance and dissonance with the chord structures above it. May also be found in voices above the bass. For a notated example see page 33.
Pentatonic scale	A five-note scale often found in folk melodies. A variety of pentatonic scales exist. Among the more popular are: C D E G A C D F G A C E F G A. These examples may be transposed to begin on any other pitch.

Perfect authentic cadence	An authentic cadence (V–I) in which the tonic note of the scale is both the highest and lowest note of the final chord (tonic).
Phrygian mode	A system of seven tones with the same arrangement of half and whole steps as from E to E on the white keys of the piano.
Pitch	The identity of a sound according to the number of vibrations produced per second. Example: A = 440 vibrations per second.
Plagal	A cadence ending with the two chords IV to I. The Amen cadence.
Quartolet	A group of four notes occurs in a measure or portion thereof normally allotted to three. This rhythmic device is usually found in meter signatures of 6/8, 6/4, 9/8, 9/4, 12/8, or 12/4. Example: In 6/8 meter the first of two beats contains four 8th notes, usually indicated with a "4" above that portion of the measure. The four notes should be played in the time span normally allotted to three.
Retardation	A suspension where the suspended note resolves up a step rather than down a step (as in the suspension).
Rhythm	Overlaying or operating within the meter, *rhythm* is a pattern of uneven durations. While the steady beats of meter combine to form measures, a rhythm creates a pattern of almost any length. Sometimes a rhythm is so simple that it is simply a duplicate of the meter—in which case the two (meter and rhythm) are synonymous.
Rhythmic repetition	Repetition of a rhythmic pattern.
Root	The pitch upon which a chord is built. Example: C E G—"C" is the root.
Root position	The arrangement of a chord when the root is the lowest sounding pitch.
Rounded binary form	A type of binary form in which the first section, or a portion thereof, usually indicated by the letter "A," is inserted near the end of the second section (letter "B"). Thus, the term *rounded* is used to indicate the return of "A" material. For more detailed information consult the *Harvard Dictionary of Music* for the term *Binary form*.
Scale	A series of ascending and/or descending pitches used to display the notes found in tonal and modal systems. For example, one of the scales displaying the pitches of the major mode is: C D E F G A B C.
Sequence	The immediate restatement of a melodic (or harmonic) figure at a higher or lower pitch so that the structure of the figure is maintained. Example— Pitches: CDE DEF EFG FGA. Each section of the sequence (CDE DEF and so on) is known as a segment (of the sequence.)
Sequence segment	The parts of the sequence. In the sequence CDE DEF EFG, CDE is the first SEGMENT, DEF is the second, and so on.
Solfeggio	Singing of melodies using the syllables: Do Re Mi Fa Sol La Ti. In the fixed-do system Do is always C, and in the movable Do system Do is the first scale degree (tonic).
Sound pattern	Any combination of tones—melodic, harmonic, or rhythmic—that form a pattern.
Stationary bass	A type of $^6_4$ (second inversion) triad where the lowest sounding tone of the chord is both approached and left by repetition. For a notated illustration see page 109.
Supertonic	Second scale degree.
Supertriplet	A triplet figure that extends beyond one beat. Example: In $^2_4$ meter, a group of three quarter notes that are intended to be performed in the time span normally allotted to the entire measure (two beats).
Suspension	A nonharmonic tone that proceeds:

note	to	same note	to	note down a step
(consonance)	to	(dissonance)	to	(consonance)
Example: C	to	C	to	B

For a notated illustration, see page 19.

Three-part form	A form most often found in homophonic music but existing as well in three-part polyphony, the first and third parts of which are either the same or nearly so. Usually designated by the letters A B A, three-part form is also known as *ternary form*.
Tonic	First scale degree.
Triad	In this text a triad is a three-note chord consisting of the interval of a major or minor 3rd and a diminished, perfect, or augmented 5th above the lowest sounding note (root). The four types of triads are:

> Major triad   =   Example: C E G
> Minor triad   =   Example: D F A
> Diminished triad   =   Example: B D F
> Augmented triad   =   Example: C E G#

Tritone	An interval comprising three whole steps—usually an augmented 4th or a diminished 5th. Example: C to F#.
Unaccented neighboring tone	A neighboring tone that is unaccented in relation to other notes of its same rhythmic value.
Unaccented passing tone	A passing tone that is unaccented in relation to other notes of its same rhythmic value. For a notated example, see page 20.
Whole tone scale	A scale made up entirely of whole steps. Example: C D E F# G# A# C.